CARNAGE:

Preventing Mass Shootings in America

Thomas Gabor
Consultant and Expert Witness
Professor of Criminology
(Retired, University of Ottawa)

BookLocker
Saint Petersburg, Florida

"But in spite of temporary victories, violence never brings permanent peace. It solves no social problem: it merely creates new and more complicated ones. It creates bitterness in the survivors and brutality in the destroyers."

Dr. Martin Luther King Jr.

Table of Contents

List of Tables

1
Mass Shootings:
Scale of the Problem

America had quite the year in 2020. The Covid-19 pandemic infected about 20 million Americans, causing widespread suffering and leaving the economy in tatters. Millions of people sought relief due to the loss of employment and more than one hundred thousand businesses failed, creating enormous housing and food insecurity. Protests demanding racial justice persisted for months in response to questionable killings of Black people—mostly men—by police. Many schools, college campuses, businesses, and other organizations were forced to operate remotely. The nation also faced a presidential impeachment and an election viewed by many as the most consequential in memory. As if these events weren't enough, mass shootings exploded in 2020, worsening the gun violence crisis that has not been addressed by federal legislation for over 25 years.

From December 14, 2012, when 20 children and 6 adults were murdered at Sandy Hook Elementary School in Newtown, Connecticut to July 2020, the Gun Violence Archive, a leading source on gun violence, has identified 2,654 mass shootings in America.[1] During that time, just three states were free of a mass shooting—North Dakota, New Hampshire, and Hawaii. Since 2013, there has been just one calendar week without a mass shooting. Mass shootings have become routine events in the US and it is not surprising to hear the young survivors of the 2018 St. Valentine's Day school shooting in Parkland, Florida refer to themselves as the "mass shooting generation."

While gun deaths in America exceed those of other advanced countries by a wide margin, mass shootings, while far too numerous, account for less than 2% of annual gun deaths.[2] Given this fact, some question why so much attention is paid by the media and activists to mass violence as opposed to gun violence in general.

The Consequences of Mass Shootings

Self-serving sensationalism is one reason for the media's special focus on mass shootings; however, the attention to these atrocities is justified by the fact that they devastate communities and our sense of safety. They have a disproportionate impact on a community and this impact may extend well beyond the affected community's boundaries. Large-scale mass shootings, in particular, may lead citizens throughout the country to reconsider attending a movie or festival, visiting a mall, or using public spaces. In fact, following two especially deadly mass shootings in Dayton, Ohio and El Paso, Texas on one weekend in August 2019, a Harris Poll found that a third of 2,000 Americans surveyed said their fear was so great they would avoid going to certain places or events.[3] Such fear has social, psychological, and economic impacts if potential customers and spectators stay home more often due to the fear of being caught in the middle of a shooting.

Perpetrators of mass shootings, whether randomly selecting victims or targeting multiple victims, also often injure and kill children and seniors who may simply be in the wrong place at the wrong time. The study conducted for this book shows that it is not uncommon for children under the age of one to be harmed in these incidents.

A 2020 survey conducted in Connecticut illustrates that mass shootings are top of mind for many people. More than 10% of that state's residents indicate that they have been, or are close to, someone who has been personally affected by a mass shooting.[4] More than 40% of residents stated that mass shootings are the violent crime they are most concerned about.

Mass shootings may have a psychological toll that is far more pronounced than what we might expect from observing the physical casualties alone. On October 16, 1991, G.

Hennard, a 35-year-old unemployed man who had been a member of the US Merchant Marines, drove his pickup truck through the front window of Luby's Cafeteria in Killeen, Texas. Armed with two semi-automatic pistols, he then proceeded to murder 23 customers and wound another 27 before killing himself. Hennard held racist views toward African Americans and Hispanics. Like a certain class of shooters, he was especially angry at women and targeted them specifically. As he was committing the mass murder, he yelled: "All women of Killeen and Belton [a neighboring city] are vipers! This is what you've done to me and my family! ...This is payback day!"[5] After being cornered by the police, Hennard fatally shot himself.

A health team assessed 136 cafeteria employees, customers, and first responders who had been at the scene in Killeen and followed them up for three years.[6] Nearly three in 10 (28%) met the criteria for post-traumatic stress disorder (PTSD). Few had a complete absence of symptoms of post-traumatic stress. One year later, 18% of those at the scene continued to display PTSD, and three years later there was no significant decline in the prevalence of PTSD among these witnesses and first responders. The lesson here is that many of those who witness a mass shooting are profoundly affected by them. The trauma extends well beyond those who are shot and can be long-term.

Another illustration of the broad impact of mass shootings is the fear experienced by high school students. An American Psychological Association survey found that, for those between 15 and 21 years of age, mass shootings constitute the greatest source of stress, with three out of four feeling anxious about the possibility of being caught in the middle of a mass or school shooting.[7] Interviews of 19-year-olds conducted by Garrett Graff for *Politico Magazine* found that many mentioned the Sandy Hook Elementary School mass shooting as the first significant news story they remember. A representative response as to the most salient events in their lives was provided by a student named Aidan, who said: "In the back of my mind, I would sit in class and I'd be like, all right, well, if something happens, how am I going to escape? Am I going to hide? Am I going to jump out a window?"[8]

Some of the measures designed to mitigate school shootings have also raised the stress levels of K-12 students. Active shooter drills have been especially stressful and controversial.[9] These drills simulate real-life attacks and, often, they involve masked men with assault rifles bursting into classrooms. Teachers may be shot at with pellet guns and children as young as five are told to cower under their desks, while others are covered with fake blood. The goal is to prepare students and teachers for real attacks, but major teachers' unions and advocacy groups want to ban the drills, arguing that they traumatize children. The president of the National Education Association notes that children wet their pants, cry, and believe they will die.[10] In some cases, following a drill, children are unable to focus in class or sleep at night.

One study compared millions of social media tweets and posts by students 90 days before and 90 days after active shooter drills were conducted.[11] Increased rates of depression and anxiety were displayed as words such as "afraid," "struggling," "nervous," "therapy," and "suicidal" were more likely to be used after the drills.

A Morning Consult poll in May 2020 found that those born from the mid-1990s (Gen Z) state that, after the coronavirus pandemic, the issue with the greatest impact on their worldview has been mass shootings, including Sandy Hook, Parkland, and Las Vegas.[12] They say that these events have had a greater impact on them than the terrorist attacks of September 11, 2001, the "Black Lives Matter" movement, and the "Me Too" movement.

Mass shootings are also very costly from an economic perspective. Gun violence costs the US an estimated $280 billion a year when direct medical costs, rehabilitation, criminal justice system costs, lost income, victim support, lost tax revenue, and quality of life costs are taken into account. These figures do not include such items as the disruption of businesses in the aftermath of a shooting.[13] Another study has found that the annual cost to the medical system alone is $170 billion, just for those gunshot wound victims requiring one major operation.[14]

Consider the mall shooting in Clackamas Town Center near Portland, Oregon in December 2012.[15] More than 150 police officers responded from 13 law enforcement agencies. The investigation lasted more than three months and produced a report nearly 1,000 pages in length. Following the shooting, the 1.5-million-square-foot mall shut down for three days during the peak of the holiday shopping season in order to calm the public, make repairs, and ramp up security. As a result, 188 stores lost revenue while the mall was closed.

Mass shootings are defined in this book as incidents in which four or more people, excluding the shooter, are shot in a single event and at one general time and location. This definition does not require that the injuries be fatal. There is some subjectivity involved with regard to the location as victims may be shot in different rooms of a house or both inside and outside a nightclub and that would still qualify here as one location. Seldom are all the victims found in the exact same spot. When victims are shot by the same suspect(s) at an entirely different location or time, that would be evidence of a spree killing.

The scale of America's problems with guns requires that we act with urgency. Over 100 Americans die from gunfire each day, and the US is a major outlier when compared with other advanced countries. For example, the US has 25 times the gun homicide rate as other high-income countries, when the incidents in these countries are combined and adjusted for population differences with the US.[16] In addition, the US, which has less than 5% of the world's population, accounts for a third of the mass shootings on the planet.[17] Unlike natural disasters, such as hurricanes and tornados, and even epidemics, gun-related deaths and injuries are not confined to specific years or seasons; nor are they transient. While there may be some seasonal variation—an issue explored in the study conducted for this book—there is a steady parade of gun homicides and mass shootings throughout the year.

The Many Types of Mass Shootings

Mass shootings are varied and often complex events. They usually defy simplistic explanations such as: "He went on a rampage because he was mentally ill," "The young man targeted his former school because he was expelled or bullied," or "The employee shot his colleagues because he was mistreated by his employer or co-workers." While these factors may help explain certain mass shootings, they are necessarily incomplete. If every mentally disturbed individual, bullied student, or disgruntled employee committed a mass shooting, America would have millions rather than a few hundred mass shootings a year. There are clearly other factors that lead a minute fraction of individuals afflicted with mental illness or unhappy at work or school to commit a massacre. There are also many shootings in which none of these factors apply.

As an illustration of how mass shootings differ, consider several high-profile events since 2007. On February 14, 2018, N. Cruz, a 19-year-old former student of Marjory Stoneman Douglas High School in Parkland, Florida, returned to his former school with an assault-style rifle and murdered 17 students and staff, wounding an additional 17. In the years leading up to the shooting, law enforcement agencies received numerous tips regarding his threatening behavior, including his desire to "shoot up a school,"[18] His online posts indicated a fascination with weapons, as well as extremist, hate-filled views toward various minority groups. Fellow students seemed to believe that if one of their peers was to commit a school shooting, it would be Cruz.

By contrast, S. Paddock, the 64-year-old man responsible for America's worst mass shooting in Las Vegas on October 1, 2017 (58 killed, 413 injured, and many more hurt due to the stampede to avoid the gunfire) offered no discernible hints of the carnage he planned to unleash. He gradually brought an arsenal of AR-10 and AR-15 rifles to his suite at the Mandalay Bay Hotel and equipped the rifles with bump stocks, which allow semi-automatics to mimic automatic weapons (machine guns) in their rate of fire. Paddock committed suicide during his assault, and extensive analysis following his death revealed no specific motive for the massacre. His brain was examined by Stanford University pathologists and revealed no abnormalities. Post-mortem investigations revealed no clear clues that would have foretold the massacre.[19]

Mental illness was a more critical factor in the shooting of 32 people at Virginia Tech University on April 16, 2007. The shooter, S. Cho, displayed numerous signs of mental illness prior to the shooting as he was diagnosed with a mood disorder, received counseling at the university, and was found by a court to be a danger to himself[20]. Cho committed suicide as his rampage was about to be ended by responding law enforcement officers. Cho, who was born in South Korea, was armed with two handguns and 19 high-capacity magazines, rather than an assault rifle. Unlike the vast majority of mass shooters, Cho released a "manifesto" that is in part incoherent and in which he railed against those who had done him harm, including "snobs," "Charlatans," and "hedonists."[21]

Another broad category of shooter includes those who target specific individuals at a workplace, in the family, or in the context of a group- or gang-related conflict. These individuals do not attack indiscriminately, although individuals not targeted may fall victim to the shooter's rage or be hit by a stray bullet or debris. On May 31, 2019, G. Martin, 45, a veteran assemblyman at Henry Pratt Company in Aurora, Illinois, shot executives at the plant upon hearing that he had been fired.[22] He then took his rage out on the plant floor, shooting at co-workers. Martin died in the incident from a police officer's bullet.

Mass shooters may also be motivated by an ideology. On December 2, 2015, S. Farook and T. Malik, a married couple, attacked a San Bernardino (California) Department of Health training event, killing 14 and injuring 22 at the scene. Farook was US-born and of Pakistani descent, whereas Malik was a green-card holder from Pakistan. According to the FBI, they were homegrown extremists inspired, but not directed, by foreign terrorist groups.[23] The couple was influenced by radical sites on the Internet and, in their communications to one another, they expressed a commitment to Islamic militancy and martyrdom. They had accumulated a large arsenal of weapons, ammunition, and bomb-making equipment in their home.

These five cases alone demonstrate the wide variety of mass shootings and the folly of seeking one explanation and prevention strategy that applies to all these events. Mass shooters are from every racial and age group, they may be psychologically stable or mentally ill, they may or may not be ideologically motivated or loners, they may select their victims carefully or be indiscriminate in picking their targets, and they vary in the type of weapons they use.

An examination of just one category of mass shooter, individuals launching school attacks, illustrates the many motives driving these individuals. Studies undertaken by the US Secret Service have found that there is no useful profile of a student attacker nor of the type of school that has been attacked.[24]

> *Attackers varied in age, gender, race, grade level, academic performance, and social characteristics. Similarly, there was no identified profile of the type of school impacted by targeted violence, as schools varied in size, location, and student-teacher ratios. Rather than focusing on a set of traits or characteristics, a threat assessment process should focus on gathering relevant information about a student's behaviors, situational factors, and circumstances to assess the risk of violence or other harmful outcomes.*

The Secret Service report is therefore telling us that, rather than trying to predict who will undertake an attack or where it will occur, the emphasis should be on assessing risks when threats or concerning behaviors occur. This guidance is based on their finding that many shooters telegraph their intentions by communicating them to peers, displaying behaviors eliciting concern, posting disturbing social media content, or acquiring firearms.

Despite our inability to predict who will attack a school, a workplace, a church, people at a gathering, or family members, determining the predisposing factors, triggers, and key contextual factors can help prevent and mitigate the impact of these shootings. For example, many school shooters have grievances with classmates or school staff, relationship issues, access to firearms, interest in violent topics, mental health or behavioral issues, and negative home life factors (e.g., a divorce). The presence of a number of these factors may warrant close scrutiny in cases in which a threat is reported and harms can be prevented by counseling and support or mitigated by ensuring that the individual posing a hazard does not have easy access to a firearm.

The Present Study

This book reports on a study, conducted by this author, of 1,029 mass shootings occurring in the US in 2019 and 2020. The analysis relied on the Gun Violence Archive, an online resource that tracks mass shootings throughout the US. The purpose of this study was to determine the annual number of and trends in mass shootings, the different categories of shootings, the locations in which they tend to occur, characteristics of suspects and victims, motives, weapons of choice, and the role of mental illness and domestic violence. Strategies to prevent the different categories of mass shootings are then proposed.

The Odds of Becoming a Victim

Table 1 illustrates the odds of being murdered in the US and selected advanced countries. It is apparent that the US stands alone, relative to other high-income countries, with regard to its rates of lethal violence. Still, the table shows that, even in the US, just one in about 29,000 people are murdered each year with a firearm. It is even more unusual for a shooting to involve more than one person. Just 10% of all homicides involve more than one victim.[25] To shoot or kill a larger number of people, preparation is more likely to be necessary and the perpetrator must have access to firearms that can fire quickly with a minimum of reloading. A certain level of shooting prowess may also be needed to shoot multiple victims. Perpetrators must also be angry enough and sufficiently callous to produce mass casualties. Furthermore, as law enforcement usually responds quickly to mass shootings, the perpetrator must be willing to risk being shot and killed by the police. These elements of mass shootings ensure that, while far too many occur in America, the odds that the average citizen will be a victim of a mass shooting is quite low, although the odds are not uniform for all segments of the population.

Table 1. Odds of Being Murdered in Selected High-Income Countries

COUNTRY AND YEAR USED FOR THE CALCULATION	# OF FIREARM HOMICIDES	ODDS OF BEING MURDERED WITH A FIREARM	ODDS OF BEING MURDERED BY ANY MEANS
USA (2014)	10,945	1 in 29,000	1 in 20,000
ISRAEL (2011)	81	1 in 95,000	1 in 51,000
CANADA (2013–2014)	131	1 in 271,000	1 in 69,000
FINLAND (2012)	17	1 in 319,000	1 in 61,000
SWITZERLAND (2013)	18	1 in 452,000	1 in 140,000
AUSTRALIA (2013)	35	1 in 655,000	1 in 106,000
SPAIN (2012)	51	1 in 918,000	1 in 129,000
GERMANY (2011)	61	<1 in 1,000,000	1 in 121,000
UK (2011–2012)	38	<1 in 1,000,000	1 in 97,000
JAPAN (2008)	11	<1 in 10,000,000	1 in 197,000

Source: Table reproduced from T. Gabor, *Confronting Gun Violence in America*, p. 8.

Unlike natural disasters and epidemics, mass shootings are intentional and thus preventable. They are not "acts of God" or natural phenomena that are difficult to control. In addition, unlike the case of pathogens, we do not become immune to gun violence. In fact, the unrelenting parade of gun deaths and mass shootings is corrosive, forcing an increasingly fearful population to remain ever-vigilant in planning their daily activities. Ultimately, the problem infects our daily lives and undermines the trust citizens have in one another. For many, this may lead to their withdrawal from social activities that would connect them to others and promote mental well-being.

Given current rates of gun mortality, if the US fails to take significant action in relation to gun violence, we can expect another half million deaths from gunfire over the next 10 years. The increasing mortality in America—close to 40,000 people died of gunfire in 2017 and 2018—and the rising death toll from mass shootings is occurring despite advances in the treatment of bullet wounds over the last two decades[26] and improvements in emergency care and response. Surgeons are telling us that they are seeing more patients with multiple bullet wounds and firearm injuries that cannot be treated.

Dr. Jeremy Cannon of the University of Pennsylvania's Perelman School of Medicine says the following about the damage produced by the high-velocity bullets fired by an AR-15 assault-type weapon: "The tissue destruction is almost unimaginable. Bones are exploded, soft tissue is absolutely destroyed. The injuries to the chest or abdomen—it's like a bomb went off."[27]

With improvements in survival rates following shootings, we would expect to see a reduction in the annual gun violence death toll. Rather, we are seeing more fatalities over the last few years than previously, suggesting that medical advances may be masking what might be an even greater increase in gun-related death had survival rates remained the same.[28] The rising mortality and volume of mass shootings point to the proliferation of weapons that are increasingly lethal, such as military-grade rifles and pistols capable of being equipped with high-capacity magazines.

The Tepid Federal Response to Gun Violence

To illustrate the scale of the problems associated with guns, consider hurricanes, which have ramped up over the last few years. Since 2016, a number of very powerful hurricanes have threatened the Atlantic Coast of the US, including, Matthew (2016), Irma (2017), and Dorian (2019). Despite the power of these storms and the potential for massive property damage, on average, 100 Americans die each year as a result of these storms. Nevertheless, in 2019, with Dorian approaching, the federal government issued emergency declarations for four states: Florida, Georgia, North and South Carolina. Contrast this with the fact that 40,000 gun deaths per year fail to elicit any such declaration nor any significant national gun legislation to deal with the gun violence scourge and its disproportionate impact on certain communities.

In addition, for over 20 years, Congressional Republicans even denied federal funds for research through the Dickey Amendment, preventing studies from proceeding on the nature and extent of gun violence, as well as policies that might prove effective in reducing it.[29] These members of Congress were acting at the behest of the gun lobby, which became panicky about research in the 1990s that was revealing the true risks associated with firearms kept in the home.

Consider the amount of federal funding for sepsis, a potentially life-threatening condition caused by the body's response to an infection. This condition kills about the same number of Americans as gun violence; however, research funding available to study it is more than one hundred times that available for gun violence.[30] With the onset of the Covid-19 pandemic, we have seen a major mobilization in the development of vaccines and trillions of dollars of relief, but we continue to see little in the way of investment in solutions to gun violence and the families and communities shattered by the problem.

The gun lobby's role in getting lawmakers to block law reforms and obstruct research is just one part of the story of why the US has failed to advance in these areas. Another part of this story is the decades-long effort by the National Rifle Association (NRA) and other gun rights organizations to promote the false narrative that guns are an effective tool for self-protection and that they are far more likely to be used to thwart criminals than as a tool to commit crimes and intimidate others, including victims of domestic violence. This campaign has succeeded in convincing most Americans that a gun in the home makes occupants safer[31] despite compelling evidence to the contrary.[32] The gun lobby's efforts have frustrated the desire of the vast majority of Americans for meaningful gun regulation.

The gun lobby has also advanced a distorted view of the Second Amendment to convince Americans that they have virtually an absolute right to own firearms that dates back to the drafting of the Constitution in the 18th century. In fact, historically, the Second Amendment was interpreted by the courts as the right to bear arms within the context of militia service only. For example, in *United States v. Miller* (1939), two defendants who had been prosecuted for failing to register and pay a tax for possessing and carrying a sawed-off shotgun across state lines argued that such requirements under the National Firearms Act violated their Second Amendment rights.[33] The US Supreme Court ultimately ruled that such a weapon had no role in an organized militia and was therefore not protected by the Second Amendment.

Following the NRA's long campaign to promote the view that the Second Amendment guaranteed a right to bear arms to individuals outside of militia service—a view characterized by former Chief Justice Warren Burger as "one of the greatest pieces of fraud on the American public"—the US Supreme Court did rule in the 2008 *Heller* decision that individuals had the right to own an operable gun in the home for protection.[34] However, writing for the majority in the 5–4 decision, Justice Antonin Scalia, a hunter and a conservative, made it clear that this right was not unlimited and that laws regulating the carrying of firearms, denying gun ownership to felons and the mentally ill, and prohibiting the carrying of dangerous and unusual weapons did not violate the Second Amendment. Court rulings since *Heller* show that the vast majority of gun laws currently being proposed do not violate the Constitution and merely require political will to pass.[35]

In fact, not only does the Constitution permit the enactment of laws regulating gun ownership, carrying, and storage, but an emerging number of scholars, including this writer, are asserting that the government's first duty is to protect its citizens.[36] The human rights group Amnesty International argues in a 2018 report, *In the Line of Fire*, that the US has breached its commitments under international human rights law. AI writes: "The USA has failed to implement a comprehensive, uniform and coordinated system of gun safety laws and regulations particularly in light of the large number of firearms in circulation, which perpetuates unrelenting and potentially avoidable violence, leaving individuals susceptible to injury and death from firearms."[37]

The human rights group asserts that nations should establish robust regulatory systems, including licensing, registration, restriction of certain weapon types, safe storage requirements, research, and policy development. Nationally, the US has done little or nothing in relation to any of these policies over the last 25 years. AI notes that countries not only have obligations to protect the life of individuals from state agents but from actual or foreseeable threats at the hands of private actors as well. Violence is especially foreseeable in low-income neighborhoods with persistently high levels of violence, poor public services, and policing that may not comply with international standards.

Organization of This Book

The primary aim of this book is to increase our understanding by discussing trends in and explanations for mass shootings, as well as by presenting the results of an analysis of mass shootings occurring in 2019 and 2020. Solutions based on the evidence and the different types of mass shootings are then presented. It is important to understand the daily shootings that occur in America. The smaller number of high-casualty, planned gun massacres (Las Vegas, Orlando, Sandy Hook, Parkland), while deserving examination in their own right, provide a misleading picture of mass shootings as a whole. The motives and measures required to prevent incidents in which a perpetrator is trying to inflict mass casualties and kill people indiscriminately are very different from more limited attacks that target specific people or that arise from spontaneous disputes. The everyday mass shootings that often occur in communities inhabited largely by people of color receive less coverage and are less likely to convey the humanity of the victims.[38]

Chapter 2 discusses the definition of mass shooting adopted in the present study and the source used to identify mass shootings occurring in 2019 and 2020, as well as the reasoning behind these choices. You will see that the choices made regarding how we define mass shootings have an enormous impact on the number of shootings we find. Chapter 3 addresses the following question: Are mass shootings becoming more frequent and lethal? The chapter also covers the factors accounting for this trend.

Chapter 4 explains the high levels of mass shootings in the US. Explanations include the high rates of gun ownership and permissive gun laws, persistent poverty, the growing rates of depression and suicide among the young, and the role of social contagion—i.e., the idea that some shooters are influenced by previous shooters and try to emulate and outdo those that have gone before them in the carnage they produce. Chapter 5 presents the findings of the study of over a thousand mass shootings occurring in 2019–2020. The chapter displays regional and state differences in the number of mass shootings; identifies the cities with the largest number of shootings; explores suspect and victim characteristics, weapons used, and the link between race and mass shootings; and examines high-casualty shootings and the settings in which they occur and the most common features/motives of shootings.

Chapters 6 and 7 present some recommendations aimed to reduce the number of shootings or at least to mitigate them. Chapter 6 focuses on societal factors other than changing gun laws, such as law enforcement initiatives, violence interruption, modifications of the physical environmental, tackling poverty, and promoting peaceful conflict resolution. Significant progress in preventing mass shootings cannot be achieved without tackling social conditions as most mass shootings are committed in environments fraught with hopelessness and danger. Chapter 7 presents solutions to mass shootings that include a licensing system for gun owners, a ban on military-style weapons, greater regulation of gun carrying, a safe storage requirement, increased regulation of dealers, and ensuring that those posing a grave danger to the community cannot acquire or possess firearms.

2
Defining a Mass Shooting

There is no one agreed-upon definition of a mass shooting. These tragedies are not alone in this respect as so many concepts lack a consensus definition and definitions may change over time and from one region or country to another. Consider concepts like poverty, obesity, and intelligence. Where does one draw the line between lower-income people and those belonging to the middle class? How much does a person of a certain height, say five feet tall, need to weigh to be considered obese? Who should we consider to be intellectually challenged? The thinking on these and so many concepts changes and is influenced by so many factors.

For example, the National Center for Children in Poverty has taken the position that a family of four with two children could be classified as "low income" if its total income fell below $48,678 in 2016.[39] This was based on what research indicates is required for the family to meet its most basic needs. However, such an income will go much further in rural Alabama than in Southern California. The cost of food, housing, transportation, available healthcare, taxes, and so many other things will determine whether such a family will truly be members of the middle class if its overall income is $49,000. The concept of poverty is therefore very complex and there is considerable disagreement about how to define "low income."

Similarly, there is no consensus as to how to define a mass shooting. The Federal Bureau of Investigation (FBI) does not define mass shootings at all but, in the 1980s, defined a mass murderer as a person who "kills four or more people in a single incident (not including himself), typically in a single location,"[40] Some sources therefore borrow from the FBI's definition and define a mass shooting as an incident involving a firearm in which four or more people are killed, not including the shooter. However, what do we make of those incidents in which fewer people are killed but many are wounded? Ignoring such cases is problematic for two reasons.

First, many survivors of gunshot wounds sustain medical conditions, including brain and spinal cord injuries, that can dramatically affect the quality of their lives. Second, significant improvements in the medical response and care of bullet wounds may reduce the number of fatalities from shootings and lead us mistakenly to believe that the threat posed by mass shootings has subsided when the reduced threat has nothing to do with a reduction in gun violence and everything to do with improvements in emergency medicine and wound care.

Other definitions range from two or more people killed or injured to four or more people killed and/or injured. One definition includes the shooter among the four injured and/or killed, while others exclude the shooter. Some definitions of mass shootings exclude domestic incidents or those that are gang-related or committed in the course of a felony (e.g., armed robbery). They take the view that we should focus only on mass shootings committed in public spaces and that involve indiscriminate killing. Such definitions exclude workplace killings and those committed in private settings, including some educational institutions. One problem with such exclusions is that we begin to make highly subjective judgments as to the motives of the shooters, and motives are not always apparent. Some shooters are killed in the course of a mass shooting, commit suicide, or refuse to cooperate with authorities. They may also not fully understand the motives that drove them to gun down a number of people. Whether indiscriminate or not, shooters can cause mass casualties. A shooting in which specific victims are targeted, such as co-workers or relatives, can kill many people and can be as harmful or traumatic as indiscriminate killings.

Shootings cannot be neatly categorized into targeted versus random incidents. They are often hybrid events. C. Whitman, the Texas Tower shooter in 1966, first murdered his wife and mother in their respective homes before ascending the tower at the University of Texas (Austin) and firing indiscriminately on students and staff on the campus below.[41] In 2012, A. Lanza murdered his mother before attacking the children and school staff at Sandy Hook Elementary School in Newtown, Connecticut.[42] In Cleveland, Texas on May 29, 2019, P. Vido, who had lived in a metal container behind a plumbing firm, shot three workers there after the firm served him with eviction papers. He also shot a sheriff's deputy who pursued him following the offense. While the perpetrator targeted the first three victims, the confrontation with the deputy was not something he planned or would have anticipated.[43]

The definitional chaos described above helps account for the wide range of findings on the nature and number of mass shootings. Where mass shootings are defined as incidents in which four people are shot, but not necessarily killed, we will find far more cases than if the definition must include four or more fatalities. In the latter case, an incident may involve dozens of people shot and would still not qualify as a mass shooting. The higher the body count required for the definition, the fewer the number of cases we will find. The majority of violent crimes have one or two victims. Fewer cases involve three victims, still fewer involve four victims, and so on. The higher the number of fatalities or casualties required before we classify an incident as a mass shooting, the fewer mass shootings we will find.

Mother Jones Magazine. To illustrate the impact of definitions of mass shootings on the number of cases identified, consider *Mother Jones* magazine, which has been tracking these shootings back to 1982. To qualify as a mass shooting for their database, an incident must have the following features:

1) The attack must be a single incident that takes place in a public space;
2) It must occur in one location, although the magazine did include several spree shootings that occurred in more than one location if they occurred within a short time frame;
3) Following the FBI's criteria, the incident must involve four or more fatalities, excluding the shooter. In 2013,

following a policy change by the Obama Administration, *Mother Jones* reduced the requirement to three or more killed;

4) The killings must be carried out by a lone shooter (although *Mother Jones* made an exception in the case of Columbine and another shooting).[44]

Mother Jones' definition also excludes mass shootings stemming from an armed robbery, gang violence, or a domestic conflict. The exceptions to its own criteria made by *Mother Jones* illustrates the difficulty of neatly defining events as a mass shooting, as there are always some events that fall just outside the established criteria. Through its restrictive criteria, *Mother Jones* has identified 118 mass shootings since 1982 and just 10 in 2019.[45]

USA Today, the Associated Press, and Northeastern University. These three sources have collaborated in tracking mass shootings. Their definition is less restrictive than *Mother Jones'* as *all* firearm incidents that meet the casualty threshold are included. However, this initiative considers a mass shooting as one involving four or more people killed. There can be more than one shooter and the shooting can take place in a private or public setting. Gang-related, as well as domestic incidents, are included. These sources found 33 mass shootings in 2019, over three times more than *Mother Jones* found.[46]

Everytown for Gun Safety. The advocacy group Everytown for Gun Safety has undertaken an analysis of mass shootings over a 10-year period covering 2009–2018. This group also defines a mass shooting as an incident involving four or more fatalities, excluding the shooter. While its analysis did not cover 2019, the group found that there was a range of between 15 and 24 mass shootings over the decade covered by its study.[47]

The Violence Project. This is a nonprofit, nonpartisan research center based in Minnesota and led by two criminologists affiliated with two universities in that state.[48] They have developed a database of mass shootings going back to 1981. The Violence Project defines a mass shooting as: "a multiple homicide incident in which four or more victims are murdered with firearms—not including the offender(s)—within one event, and at least some of the murders occurred in a public location or locations in close geographical proximity...." The Project's definition excludes murders attributable to any other underlying criminal activity or commonplace circumstance (armed robbery, criminal competition, insurance fraud, argument, or romantic triangle). With all the exclusions, it is not surprising that this definition yielded a small number of cases. A total of seven mass shootings were identified in 2019.[49]

Gun Violence Archive (GVA). This source has been tracking mass shootings since 2013.[50] The GVA is maintained by professional staff and defines a mass shooting as an incident in which four or more people (excluding the shooter) are shot and/or killed in a single incident at the same general time and location. The GVA does not require that victims be killed for an incident to be classified as a mass shooting. It also includes shootings motivated by gang-related disputes and those of a domestic nature. In addition, the GVA includes shootings in a private setting. With this more inclusive definition, the GVA uncovered 417 mass shootings in 2019.[51]

The Mass Shooting Tracker (MST). This source, also initiated in 2013, is a crowd-sourced database verified by managers of the website.[52] Like the GVA, the MST is updated daily. It too defines a mass shooting as an incident in which four or more people are shot, but not necessarily killed. However, unlike most of the other databases, the perpetrator is included in the count. This inclusion of the perpetrator makes it more likely that incidents reach the threshold of four victims. As a result, the MST yields a higher count than the others. In 2019, the MST did not complete its count of mass shootings but, as of August 4, uncovered 294 cases. By contrast, the GVA identified 250 mass shootings by that date.

The Stanford Mass Shootings of America (MSA). This data project was initiated in 2012 in reaction to the slaughter of students and staff at Sandy Hook Elementary School in Newtown, Connecticut.[53] A product of the Stanford Geospatial Center, MSA defined a mass shooting as involving three or more shooting victims (not necessarily fatalities), not including the shooter. Identifiably gang-, drug-, or organized crime-related shootings were not included in the database. While the MSA set a lower threshold of three persons shot, the exclusion of gang- or crime-related incidents brought the number of mass shootings identified below that of the GVA and the MST. Due to the significant resource requirements involved in maintaining its database, Stanford has permanently suspended its work.

Louis Klarevas, Columbia University. Professor Klarevas has focused his attention on the most serious mass shootings—high-fatality gun massacres.[54] He defines a gun massacre as an incident in which six or more people are killed by firearms, excluding the shooter. He does not exclude incidents committed in private or in the process of committing a crime. Klarevas identified 111 attacks between 1966 and 2015. There were seven of these massacres in 2015.[55] Until 2015, no other year dating back to 1966 had seen more than five gun massacres.

Table 2 provides a summary of recent sources that have tracked mass shootings.

Table 2. Sources that have Tracked Mass Shootings

DATABASE	CASUALTY THRESHOLD	LOCA-TION	INCLUDES/EXCLUDES	NUMBER OF CASES IDENTIFIED
MOTHER JONES	Three or more killed, excluding the shooter	In a public space	Excludes gang-related and domestic cases	10 (2019)
USA TODAY, AP, NORTH-EASTERN U.	Four or more killed, excluding the shooter	Public or private setting	All motives are included	33 (2019)
EVERYTOWN FOR GUN SAFETY	Four or more killed, excluding the shooter	Public or private setting	All motives are included	19 per year, 2009–2018
THE VIOLENCE PROJECT	Four or more killed, excluding the shooter	In a public space	Excludes crime-related, domestic, or other disputes	7 (2019)
GUN VIOLENCE ARCHIVE	Four or more shot and/or killed, excluding the shooter	Public or private setting	All motives are included	417 (2019)
MASS SHOOTING TRACKER	Four or more shot and/or killed, including the perpetrator	Public or private setting	All motives are included	497 (2019) – No. based on August 4 total
STANFORD MASS SHOOTINGS IN AMERICA	Three or more shot, excluding the shooter	Public or private setting	Excluded gang-, drug-, organized-crime cases	Discontinued 65 incidents in 2015
LOUIS KLAREVAS (COLUMBIA U.)	Gun massacres—six or more killed, excluding the shooter	Public or private setting	All motives are included	Completed; 7 incidents in 2015

Table 2 illustrates the wide range of research findings depending on the definition adopted. For example, while The Violence Project identified a total of seven mass shootings in 2019 due to a highly restrictive definition, the Mass Shooting Tracker was on a path to identifying nearly 500 mass shootings due to a far more inclusive definition. Such a definitional morass hardly provides guidance to policy-makers as to the nature and gravity of the problem. The low figure yielded by The Violence Project might lead one to conclude that mass shootings are very infrequent events that do not merit much attention on the part of lawmakers and researchers. On the other hand, the broader definitions adopted by the Mass Shooting Tracker and Gun Violence Archive yield mass shooting figures that suggest that America is in the midst of a profound crisis with regard to gun violence.

Daniel Webster, a professor at the Bloomberg School of Public Health at Johns Hopkins University, and his associates have called for a uniform definition of mass shooting to address the definitional chaos so that policies can be based on a body of comparable research. They write:

With this in mind, we advocate for a definition of 4 or more casualties, without a restriction on location of incident or whether the incident had gang or drug involvement. Databases that define mass shootings by victim fatalities—rather than total number of victims injured or killed—fail to capture the injury caused when people survive gun violence. Individuals who are nonfatally shot in these incidents are discounted, though they may suffer physical and psychological traumas for the remainder of their lives. Restricting incidents to those that occurred in a public place undercounts the true number of events that result in mass shooting casualties, especially domestic violence incidents that occur in the home. We also urge researchers not to exclude incidents that appear to be gang- or drug-related because uninvolved bystanders are still being killed or injured in these events. If we fail to count gang- and drug-related incidents, then these incidents will be less likely to receive the same attention in terms of prevention efforts. For these reasons, we urge the federal government to establish a mass shooting definition of 4 or more casualties, excluding the perpetrator, regardless of place or gang- and/or drug-involvement.[56]

This author agrees with the reasoning of Webster and his colleagues. Therefore, for the purposes of the present study, the Gun Violence Archive has been chosen as the source for identifying mass shootings. It makes little sense to exclude incidents in which multiple people are shot but have survived. Consider an incident that occurred in Gilroy, California on July 28, 2019. A shooter armed with an AK-47 assault weapon opened fire at a garlic festival, killing three people and wounding another 17.[57] In another case, a shooting at a block party in Washington, DC on August 9, 2020 ended with one person dead and 21 others wounded.[58] It is believed that four shooters were involved in this incident and over 100 shots were fired. These high-profile, high-casualty incidents would not be considered to be mass shootings if the definition only covered incidents with four or more fatalities. Frankly, it makes little sense to consider as a mass shooting an incident with four fatalities and no victims, while excluding an incident like the shootings in Gilroy and Washington in which a large number of victims sustained serious injuries and the communities were severely traumatized.[59]

In addition, sources excluding shootings that do not occur in public and that do not involve indiscriminate killing (*Mother Jones*, The Violence Project) suggest that such killings are more serious or traumatic than those that are gang-related or occur at a workplace, in the home, or at some form of social gathering. There is no evidence that this is the case. In addition, even where victims are targeted or known to the offender, other persons not known to the shooter and not targeted are frequently caught in the crossfire.

Excluding shootings due to the perceived motives of the shooter is also a highly subjective exercise. Simply because someone is thought to be affiliated with a gang does not mean that every action on his part is committed on behalf of the gang. He may be acting on a personal motive in a particular instance. In fact, neighborhood cliques today allow for more autonomy of action than more traditional, hierarchical gangs in which members wait to receive instructions from their leaders. In addition, shooters may target someone at a gathering and end up killing uninvolved people, including young children. This happens far too frequently. Should this be classified as a targeted shooting or an indiscriminate one? We also see cases that start out as a domestic homicide and spill over into another environment. The shooter who murdered 20 children and six school staff at Sandy Hook Elementary School in Newtown in 2012 first killed his mother and went on to indiscriminately shoot those at the school. Events often do not fall neatly into one category, such as domestic, targeted, or random.

To the victims and their families, the motives of shooters matter little relative to the suffering inflicted. The physical injuries, the loss of loved ones, the disabilities, loss of one's quality of life, and level of income override any concern about whether the shooter targeted his victims or fired indiscriminately into a crowd, belonged to a gang, or had some form of psychological infirmity. The motives of the shooter also do not significantly affect the economic costs of shootings incurred by the medical and justice systems.

In addition to sharing its definition of a mass shooting, the Gun Violence Archive (GVA) has been selected as the source for the study described in this book due to its thorough and professional approach to identifying and describing each incident. The GVA is managed by professional staff who examine 2,500 law enforcement and media sources every day. For each event that meets their definition of a mass shooting, they record information on a number of variables including:

- the city/town and state in which the offense occurred;
- the number of individuals shot and killed;
- the age and gender of the alleged perpetrators and victims;

- the location and circumstances of the offense; and,
- the weapons used.

The GVA includes shootings both in public and private settings. It also does not exclude incidents on the basis of the motives. For each mass shooting, the GVA provides a minimum of one and usually several links to media stories on the incident and often provides a link to a description of the offense furnished by the law enforcement agency with jurisdiction over the case. The GVA tends to provide more detail on each incident than other sources.

Table 3 lists the key issues addressed by the present study.

Table 3. Key Questions Tackled in This Study

- Are mass shootings occurring more often and are they becoming more lethal?
- In which regions and states are mass shootings most likely to occur?
- Do mass shootings usually occur in large urban centers?
- Are mass shootings most likely to occur in certain locations (e.g., parks, nightclubs, the street, schools, homes)?
- What are the different categories or types of mass shootings, given the varying motives and circumstances?
- How important are factors like mental illness, gangs, and domestic violence?
- Has the Covid-19 pandemic had an impact on the number of mass shootings?
- What proportion occurs in schools or on college/university campuses?
- Are certain gender, age, or racial groups more likely to be the victims of mass shootings?
- Are certain weapons more likely to be used?

- How often are guns used by victims to defend themselves during mass shootings?
- Do states with tougher gun laws have fewer mass shootings?
- What strategies are available to prevent mass shootings or, at least, to mitigate the harm produced by them?

3
Trends in Mass Shootings

While adopting different definitions of mass shootings and varying time frames, a number of studies point in the same direction: Mass shootings are becoming more frequent and more lethal.

A study by the Congressional Research Service examined public shootings in which four or more people were killed over a 44-year period from 1970 to 2013.[60] The study found that, with the exception of the 1990s, when the average number of fatalities per incident declined modestly, these events became more frequent and lethal over time (Table 4). When fatal and nonfatal injuries were considered, casualties nearly doubled from 7.5 per incident in the 1970s to 13.7 per incident in the 2010s.

Table 4. The Number and Severity of Public Mass Shootings from 1970-2013

YEARS	INCIDENTS PER YEAR	VICTIMS MURDERED PER INCIDENT
1970-79	1.1	5.5
1980-89	2.7	6.1
1990-99	4.0	5.6
2000-09	4.1	6.4
2010-2013	4.5	7.4

Source: Congressional Research Service

My own analysis in *Confronting Gun Violence in America* pointed in the same direction.[61] I used *Mother Jones'* list of mass shootings from 1982–2015. This source also focused on public shootings as opposed to domestic, felony, or gang-related incidents. The analysis showed that the number of mass shootings per year more than doubled from the 1980s and 1990s to the 2000s. From 2010 to 2015, the number of cases per year nearly doubled once again from the 1990s and 2000s and more than quadrupled from the annual number of cases in the 1980s. Total fatalities per year increased each decade, but the number of fatalities per shooting was highest in the 1980s. This situation was due to the impact of two very large mass killings on the relatively small number of incidents in the 1980s. It may also be the case that lower-casualty mass shootings in the more distant past and the pre-Internet era may be missed more often than high-casualty shootings, thereby artificially raising the average number of fatalities per incident.

The cable news network CNN has examined the country's deadliest mass shootings over a 70-year period from 1949 to 2019.[62] Those shootings in which 10 or more victims were killed were included. The list did not include domestic and gang-related incidents. Of the 26 mass shootings identified, 13 (50%) took place in the last 10 years and 17 or nearly two out of three occurred since 2007.

Louis Klarevas of Columbia University traced gun massacres in which six or more victims died back to 1966, the year in which C.Whitman, the former Marine sharpshooter, climbed up to the observation deck atop the University of Texas Tower in Austin and opened fire, killing 14 people and wounding 31 on the campus below.[63] Klarevas found that the number of gun massacres fluctuated within a narrow range (15–22 per 10-year period) over the first four decades of his study (1966–75, 1976–85, 1986–95, and 1996–2005). However, the number of these incidents increased dramatically to 39 from 2006–2015. He found that the death toll per incident also increased steadily over time, with the exception of 1996–2005. During 1966–75, an average of about seven people were killed per massacre. This number rose to an average of nine fatalities from 2006–2015. Klarevas' study showed that the number and lethality of high-casualty mass shootings have risen, especially from the mid-2000s.

The finding that the number of mass shootings has risen and that many of the deadliest mass shootings have occurred in the last decade or so is striking in light of significant improvements in the medical response and treatment of bullet wounds over the last 70 years. As an illustration of improving survival rates, an Indiana study conducted in the 1970s found that mortality rates for gunshot wounds to the abdomen declined sharply over time. These rates fell from 60% in the 1930s to 13% by the 1960s. [64] Thus, survival rates during that time more than doubled (from 40% to 87%).

More recently, emergency room doctors who treat individuals with gunshot and knife wounds indicate that survival rates have risen due to the spread of hospital trauma centers, the increased use of helicopters to transport patients, improved training of first responders, and lessons learned from the battlefields of Iraq and Afghanistan. C. William Schwab, a surgeon and director of the Firearm and Injury Center at the University of Pennsylvania, states that many more people are being saved than was the case just 10 years ago.

To illustrate, data from the Centers for Disease Control and Prevention's (CDC's) National Electronic Injury Surveillance System-All Injury Program show that serious assaults by gunfire requiring a hospital stay rose by 47 % to 30,759 in 2011 from 20,844 in 2001.[65] For the same years, homicides in the US declined by about 20% from 15,980 in 2001 to 12,664 in 2011. Thus, despite a large increase in serious injuries by firearm, the mortality rate declined.

Andrew Peitzman, chief of general surgery and trauma services at the University of Pittsburgh Medical Center, notes that trauma doctors have revolutionized the care of gunshot wounds over the last 30 years.[66] Peitzman adds that the typical shooting of 30 years ago often involved a .22-caliber Saturday Night Special, while the common shooting today involves a

9mm semiautomatic pistol, which has larger bullets and can fire more quickly. The typical shooting victim today has at least three bullet wounds.

Whether it is due to a larger number of motivated offenders or more lethal weapons, or some combination of the two, it is clear that despite improvements in the medical response and treatments, deaths continue to rise. The medical advances are masking what would otherwise be even a more serious situation.

More immediate trends provide little comfort as mass shootings seem to have become a daily occurrence in America and there are days when multiple incidents occur. Table 5 shows that mass shootings, as defined in this study, have increased noticeably from 2014. In 2014, the Gun Violence Archive recorded 269 mass shootings. From 2015 to 2018, the number of mass shootings fluctuated between 335 and 382 incidents per year—about one incident per day. In 2019, mass shootings reached a new level, with 417 incidents in a single year—more than one per day. In 2020, the record number of mass shootings reached in 2019 was obliterated. The record number of 417 reached in 2019 was reached on September 3, 2020, after just eight months of the year had elapsed. A total of 612 mass shootings was recorded for 2020, an increase over 2019 of 46.8% and more than double the number of cases seen in 2014. On July 5, 2020, there were 15 mass shootings and few days went by in 2020 without at least one mass shooting.

Table 5. Trends in Mass Shootings in America—2014–2020

YEAR	# OF MASS SHOOTINGS
2014	269
2015	335
2016	382
2017	346
2018	337
2019	417
2020	612

Source: Gun Violence Archive

The Covid-19 pandemic has had a marked impact on mass shootings. Looking at Table 6, we see that as of the end of March 2020, the month in which many states began to lock down, there were just four more cases in 2020 than in 2019 (71 to 67). In the initial wave of the pandemic, the largest number of states had stay-at-home and related orders during the month of April.[67] Given the restrictions, it is not surprising that the number of mass shootings declined from 2019 to 2020 during that month (33 to 26). By the end of May 2020, many states had begun to ease their restrictions and the number of mass shootings again exceeded those in 2019, but not by a wide margin (62 to 48).

The increase in mass shootings in 2020 could not be accounted for by the normal seasonal uptick in these incidents. From January to May 2019, there was an average of just under 30 mass shootings per month, while in the same months of 2020 there was an average of 31 mass shootings per month. In the summer months of 2019 (June to August), mass shootings averaged 45 cases per month, a 52% increase from January to May of that year. However, in 2020, there was a 177% increase in cases from the first five months of the year to the summer months (31 to 86 cases). Thus, seasonal variations could not account for the near tripling of mass shootings from June to August 2020. In the summer of 2020, there was an astounding average of nearly three mass shootings per day!

Table 6. Number of Mass Shootings by Month, 2019 and 2020

MONTH	2019	2020
JANUARY	27	25
FEBRUARY	20	21
MARCH (2020 LOCKDOWNS BEGIN)	20	25
APRIL	33	26
MAY (2020 LOCKDOWNS LIFTING)	48	62
JUNE	53	95
JULY	42	88
AUGUST	40	78
SEPTEMBER	34	67
OCTOBER	33	51
NOVEMBER	32	50
DECEMBER	34	25
TOTAL	416*	613*

Source: Gun Violence Archive

*May be slight variation from GVA's website as they may add or delete a case if information becomes available that changes its status as a mass shooting

Just as many states were emerging from their lockdowns, a second major issue that has long dogged this country came to the fore on May 25, 2020. That evening in Minneapolis, Minnesota, George Floyd, an African American man recently unemployed due to the pandemic, was purchasing cigarettes with what the clerk believed was a counterfeit $20 bill.[68] The young clerk called police and two officers arrived. By that time, Floyd was sitting in a car nearby with two other people. Officer Thomas Lane approached the vehicle, pulled out his gun, and instructed Floyd to show his hands. Lane pulled Floyd out of the car and, subsequently, Floyd resisted being handcuffed. Once handcuffed, he became compliant, as he had been when the police initially approached his vehicle. A struggle did occur when officers tried to put Floyd in their squad car.

Officer Derek Chauvin arrived at the scene and he and other officers were involved in a further attempt to put Floyd in the police car. Floyd complained he was claustrophobic and Chauvin pulled Floyd away from the passenger side, causing him to fall to the ground, where he lay face down, still in handcuffs. This is when witnesses began to film Floyd, who appeared to be in a distressed state. While restrained by officers, Chauvin placed his left knee between Floyd's head and neck. For just under eight minutes, Chauvin kept his knee on Floyd's neck. Transcripts obtained from bodycams worn by the officers showed Floyd complained over 20 times that he could not breathe. He pleaded for his mother and begged for his life. He knew that he was about to die.

The killing of George Floyd by police was met with revulsion by Americans of every race and ignited protests throughout the country. The frustration and economic suffering spawned by the pandemic-related lockdowns, as well as the anger and despair brought on by the killing of Floyd and several other African Americans by the police, were powerful factors in the surge of mass shootings seen in the summer and fall of 2020. Chapter 4 discusses these and other factors shaping the US's status as a global outlier in its high volume of mass shootings.

4

Explaining Mass Shootings
in the United States

The US has 4% of the world's population but a third of all the mass shootings. How do we explain America's standing as a world leader in civilian mass shootings? In addition, how do we explain the continuing surge in mass shootings in this country?

One popular belief is that the US has more gun deaths and mass shootings simply because it is a more violent society. According to this belief, it is our culture of violence, not our higher levels of gun ownership, that explains why we see more mass shootings. Others attribute our problems with gun violence to mental illness and even violent video games. This chapter examines the role of mental illness in gun violence.

As for the argument that America has more homicide due to a higher cultural propensity toward crime and violence and not due to the widespread possession of guns, legal scholars Franklin Zimring and Gordon Hawkins have shown, in their seminal book *Crime Is Not the Problem*, that the US does not in fact stand out as more violent or crime-prone relative to other advanced countries.[69] Where it stands out is in its levels of lethal violence. Zimring and Hawkins show that burglary and theft rates in the US are comparable to those in other Western, developed countries. The US has about the same level of ordinary crimes as many other nations. In fact, people living in Australia, New Zealand, and Canada are more likely to be victims of assault.

However, when it comes to lethal violence, the US stands alone with a rate of criminal homicide that is many times that of most affluent countries. Zimring and Hawkins state that American violence is so dangerous due to the widespread availability of guns: "Firearms use is so prominently associated

39

with the high death rate from violence that starting with any other topic would rightly be characterized as an intentional evasion."[70]

As is also the case with many mass shootings, Zimring and Hawkins note that close to a third of American homicides arise from arguments rather than crimes. Gun possession and use is an obvious reason why arguments in America turn deadly as the majority of homicides involve guns. Guns are used in 4% of all index (major) crimes, 20% of all violent crimes, and 70% of all homicides, illustrating the association between gun use and homicide. While the US has 3.7 times the *non-gun* murder rate of England and Wales, it has 63 times the *gun* murder rate of these countries, resulting in an overall murder rate (gun and non-gun) that is 8.5 times that of England and Wales. This situation demonstrates the extent to which the gap in homicides between the US and England/Wales is elevated by the frequent presence of guns in the US when disputes occur.[71]

Impact of High Gun Ownership Levels in the US

America has the largest civilian arsenal of firearms in the world. According to the international Small Arms Survey conducted in 2017, the US has an estimated 393 million firearms in private hands, which amounts to 120 guns for every 100 people.[72] This arsenal accounts for up to half of all civilian-owned guns on the planet. In the first 10 months of 2020, Americans purchased a record 17 million firearms, in response to the uncertainty prompted by the pandemic and the protests for racial justice.[73]Firearm purchases also surged after the Capitol Hill revolt and inauguration of a Democratic president in January 2021.[74]

International comparisons show that countries with higher levels of gun ownership have higher rates of gun violence. This writer's analysis of 32 high-income countries shows that those with higher gun ownership levels tend to have higher rates of gun homicide.[75] Other than Estonia, with unstable figures due to its small population and just a few dozen homicides a year, the US stands alone with both the highest rates of gun homicide and gun ownership among high-income countries.

Within the US, studies show that gun-related deaths increase with ownership. Mass shootings increase in states with higher gun ownership levels. Emma Fridel of Florida State University examined mass shootings that occurred from 1991 to 2016.[76] She found a strong link between gun ownership levels and mass shootings. States with the lowest gun ownership levels experienced mass shootings about every four and a half years, whereas those with the highest ownership levels experienced such shootings about every 15 months.

Paul Reeping of Columbia University and his associates found that every 10% increase in household gun ownership was associated with a 35% increase in the number of mass shootings in a state.[77] Reeping and his colleagues also ranked state gun laws with regard to their permissiveness. They found that a 10-unit increase in the permissiveness of state gun laws was associated with an 11.5% higher rate of mass shootings. A study by GVPedia found that, between 2013 and 2019, states rated as having weak gun laws had 4.7% more shootings, 50.3% more deaths, and 18.4% more overall casualties than states with strong gun laws. High-fatality shootings (six-plus people killed) occur 53.3% more often in states with weaker gun laws and are more lethal, with an average of four more people dying per incident.[78]

The Proliferation of Highly Lethal Firearms and Ammunition

Mass shootings are facilitated by firearms and high-capacity ammunition magazines that enable the murder and wounding of large numbers of people in a short time span. Assault rifles and even pistols equipped with high-capacity magazines can turn killings into massacres. On August 4, 2019, C. Betts shot 26 people, nine fatally, in under 30 seconds in Dayton, Ohio's

Oregon entertainment district.[79] He used an AR-15 style firearm, a weapon originally designed for the military, with a shortened barrel along with a drum magazine holding 100 rounds of ammunition.

In fact, many of the worst massacres in recent history have been committed with the help of military-style weapons. In America's worst civilian mass shooting on October 1, 2017, S. Paddock opened fire on concertgoers from a Las Vegas hotel on the Strip, shooting nearly 500 people, 58 fatally. Over 300 more were trampled or injured in the ensuing chaos. The shooter was armed with close to two dozen AR-15 and AR-10 type rifles, and 10 100-round drum magazines. In addition, the AR-15 rifles were equipped with bump stocks, a feature that allows a firearm to mimic one that is fully automatic, resulting in more rapid firing. The country's next worst mass shooting took place in Orlando on June 12, 2016. That evening, O. Mateen opened fire inside a gay nightclub, killing 49 and wounding another 53 people. He also used an assault-style weapon, the Sig Sauer MCX semi-automatic rifle, as well as a pistol. Other high-casualty shootings in which assault-style weapons have been used include the Sandy Hook Elementary School shooting in Newtown, Connecticut (26 dead, two wounded), the Aurora, Colorado theater shooting (12 dead, 58 wounded), the San Bernardino, California terrorist attack (14 killed, 22 injured), the Sutherland Springs, Texas church shooting (26 killed, 20 injured), the El Paso, Texas Walmart shooting (23 killed, 23 wounded), the Dayton shooting, and many others.

Everytown for Gun Safety, an advocacy group that conducts research, has found that shootings committed with assault weapons and/or high-capacity magazines produce more deaths and injuries than other weapons, exposing the myth behind the slogan: "Guns don't kill people, people kill people."[80] Aside from the motivation and the skills of the shooter, the type of weapon used has an independent effect on the number and type of casualties. From 2013 to 2019, of the top 20 highest-casualty mass shootings, 14 were committed with assault weapons.[81]

Many factors determine the impact of a weapon on the shooting victim, including a bullet's mass, velocity, and composition. The AR-15, for example, fires lightweight, high-speed bullets that are designed to tumble on impact, causing grievous wounds usually seen only on battlefields. In addition, certain forms of ammunition, such as hollow-point bullets, are designed to expand or fragment upon impact, creating wider wound channels.

Nobody is more qualified to comment on the increased danger of these weapons than surgeons who witness the damage firsthand. Dr. Jeremy Cannon is with the University of Pennsylvania's Perelman School of Medicine and has served in Iraq and Afghanistan. He says the following about the injuries sustained from an AR-15 rifle: "The tissue destruction is almost unimaginable. Bones are exploded, soft tissue is absolutely destroyed. The injuries to the chest or abdomen—it's like a bomb went off."[82]

Dr. Martin Schreiber of the Oregon Health and Science University also served in Iraq and Afghanistan. He points out that bullets from an AR-15 leave the rifle at a velocity of over 3,000 feet per second, while bullets from common handguns travel at a third or half of that speed. The resulting impact on the human body is exponentially greater. Schreiber states: "You will see multiple organs shattered. The exit wounds can be a foot wide. I've seen people with entire quadrants of their abdomens destroyed."[83]

Assault-style rifles have become increasingly popular. Through a combination of mass shootings, which gave the AR-15 style rifle growing notoriety, and bans that gave it more attention, it has become the most popular rifle in the country.[84] Another trend contributing to lethal violence and mass shootings has been the development of high-caliber handguns. By the 1980s, plastics had been developed to withstand the energy produced by high-caliber rounds. High-caliber pistols fire .40 and .45 caliber rounds, bullets that are close to a half inch in radius and about twice as large as the more conventional .22. A significant proportion of handguns used in crime fire high-caliber rounds.[85]

Police Chief Richard Biehl of Dayton, Ohio had the following to say about the futility of the rapid response by his officers to the 2019 shooting in the city's Oregon District:

Despite their best efforts, their heroic efforts, their extraordinarily rapid response to this horrific threat doing what has really rarely been done anywhere in the country to stop a threat that soon and still nine dead and 20 others injured.... It's amazing the harm a person can cause in such an extraordinarily short period of time when they have a high-velocity weapon with an enormous amount of ammunition.... There's a balance between protecting oneself and providing weapons and equipment that allows mass shootings to occur and for victims to be injured or killed at a rate of more than 1 per second, which happened in the Oregon district.... That's unconscionable and that's something that can't be deemed reasonable.[86]

Anthony Braga of Northeastern University and Philip Cook of Duke University examined a sample of fatal and nonfatal shootings that occurred in Boston from 2010 to 2014.[87] They compared shootings involving small-, medium-, and large-caliber firearms. They found clear evidence that the size of ammunition used made a difference in the outcome. When a small round (.22) was used, 30% of the shootings were fatal. When a medium-size round (9mm or .35 inches) was used, 57% of the shootings were fatal. When a large round (.357 Magnum) was used, 72% of the shootings were fatal. Firearm caliber was not linked to the number or location of wounds, or circumstances of the assault, indicating that shooter intent did not vary by the caliber of the weapon used. The researchers therefore concluded that it was the caliber of the firearm and not the motives of the perpetrators that accounted for the differences in the outcome of the cases.

Permissive Gun Laws

While they vary from state to state, gun laws in the US overall are much weaker than they are in other high-income countries. At both the federal level and in most states, the US lacks a licensing system that would perform a comprehensive screening to assess a person's suitability for gun ownership before he or she could purchase a firearm. NICS, the national instant background check system, has major loopholes and limitations. Private gun transfers, accounting for at least 25% of all gun sales or transfers, whether conducted through the internet, gun shows, or personal networks, do not require a background check at all. This means that those prohibited from firearm ownership as a result of a felony conviction, mental illness, domestic violence, or other disqualifying condition can get around the prohibition by purchasing a gun on the private market.

Weak Screening of Owners. Even where it occurs, the standard federally mandated background check typically involves a two-minute call by a gun dealer to the FBI or state point of contact who then searches three databases to determine whether an individual falls in a prohibited category. If not, the sale can proceed. Where an alert is found, the FBI has three business days to make the case for denying the sale. If they fail to do so, even an alert on the file cannot stop the sale from proceeding. This is known as the Charleston loophole, after the 2015 mass shooting at the Emanuel African Methodist Episcopal Church in Charleston, South Carolina. The background check revealed an alert next to the shooter's name but the FBI could not find the disqualifying drug-related conviction in time. He was therefore able to purchase the handgun he used in the shooting. Another problem is that many states do not forward relevant criminal, mental health, and drug-related information to the FBI. Thus, background checks are often conducted with incomplete records.

Nationally, there is no interview with prospective gun buyers; no reference checks with family members, co-workers, or others acquainted with the buyer; no education and training in the law, marksmanship, and gun safety; and no competency tests evaluating one's knowledge of firearms, the law, or one's skills with a firearm.

Inadequate Controls of Assault-Style Weapons. Nationally, there is no ban on weapons of war, such as the AR-15 style rifle, and just a handful of states ban these weapons. It is estimated that there are about 15 million of these firearms in the hands of American civilians. Assault weapons are used in a significant proportion of mass shootings, raise the lethality of shootings, increase the likelihood that bystanders will be shot in targeted shootings, and are often used in the murder of police officers.[88]

Inadequate Regulation and Accountability of the Gun Industry. The regulation of the gun industry in the US makes it clear that public safety takes a back seat to the commercial interests of this industry. Unlike virtually every other consumer product, such as toys, appliances, and even mattresses, the Consumer Product Safety Commission has been expressly forbidden by Congress from regulating firearms or ammunition. This agency's mission is to protect the public from unreasonable risks of injury, develop safety standards, and conduct research into product-related illness and injury.[89] As a result, no agency can ensure that guns do not explode in the user's hand or discharge when dropped, and manufacturers are not required to equip all guns with features, such as loaded chamber indicators, that minimize accidents by owners who mistakenly believe that a gun is not loaded.[90]

In 2005, following a pressure campaign by the NRA, a national law, The Protection of Lawful Commerce in Arms Act (PLCAA), was passed and signed into law by President George W. Bush. This law effectively shields the firearms industry from liability when harms are committed with its products. With a few exceptions, families of those perishing in mass shootings, for example, are no longer able to sue gunmakers for producing the weapons used in these horrors. The PLCAA essentially removed the industry's accountability for harms enabled by firearms they manufacture and sell.

Permissive Right-to-Carry Laws. America's laws relating to the carrying of firearms stand out relative to other countries. Since the 1980s, many states have expanded right-to-carry laws. In over half the states, authorities have little or no discretion and must issue a permit to carry a firearm unless the applicant falls in a specific prohibited category (e.g., he/she has been convicted of a felony, is a domestic abuser, mentally ill, or has been dishonorably discharged from the military). Another 15 states allow people to carry guns with no permit at all.[91] Millions of Americans carry guns, leading to the possible escalation of ordinary disputes to lethal violence. Many mass shootings documented in this book involve the casual carrying of guns that are deployed when an altercation breaks out in a bar, home gathering, or park.

Right-to-carry laws have increased state homicide rates by an average of 13%-15%.[92] In addition, the Washington-based Violence Policy Center has found that, from May 2007 to April 2020, concealed gun permit holders were involved in 1,371 homicide and suicide incidents, including 35 mass shootings and the killing of 24 law enforcement officers.[93] This situation reflects the poor screening and training received in most states by those who hold permits to carry firearms. In states where training is required it is often very cursory.

Just half of all states require the firing of a weapon as part of the permitting process. As an illustration of the inadequate education and training in many states, consider Florida, the state that pioneered the modern permissive "shall issue" laws and that has more concealed weapons permit holders than any other—over 2.2 million as of December 31, 2020.[94] Permit holders in Florida have a criminal record check and must complete a gun safety course (with some exceptions), submit an application, and get fingerprinted.

Florida Statutes Chapter 790.06 does not spell out the contents of the course; it merely indicates the qualifications the instructors must possess (e.g., certification by the NRA or the Department of Florida Fish and Wildlife) or the organizations that may offer the course. It does not specify whether the course needs to include instruction on the safe handling of firearms, when it is appropriate to use lethal force against another person, what constitutes good judgment (when to shoot/not to shoot), how to hold and load a gun, and the extent to which the course should teach marksmanship.

The three-hour course taken by this writer involved classroom instruction (although an insurance product was pitched for about 20 minutes), and the rest of the course involved waiting for and ultimately taking five shots with a handgun at a firing range. During the class, the instructor handed out literature offering one-on-one courses in shooting fundamentals, handling skills, and maintenance/cleaning of guns, implying that the concealed weapons course did not cover gun handling or shooting fundamentals. The course contents were very basic, covering the use of force, gun safety basics, and the settings into which the applicant can bring a gun. There was no shooting accuracy requirement to complete the course. Nor was there any test of gun handling, information retention, or training on judgment, whether through simulators or real-world exercises. In the course taken by this writer, everyone passes regardless of what they have learned and how they do on the firing range.

An especially troubling aspect of firearms training in Florida, as well as in most states, is that training is provided by private businesses rather than law enforcement. Operators have a financial interest in passing everyone as these will be future customers for their gun store or firing range. In other countries, law enforcement is responsible for these courses, has more rigorous standards, and is not afraid to fail people if they do not demonstrate a specified level of competence.

Stand Your Ground Laws. The permissive carry laws in many states, combined with Stand Your Ground (SYG) laws that have been enacted in a majority of states, form a toxic brew that has enabled many killings in the US. While they vary, SYG laws tend to give individuals the right to use deadly force when they have a "reasonable belief" that they are facing death or serious injury.[95] Under these laws, no actual attack is necessary to justify the use of force, including lethal force. A person who has provoked someone or instigated a conflict and uses lethal force may still be granted immunity from prosecution if the person they have provoked responds violently to the provocation. Under SYG laws, there is no duty to retreat or to solve a dispute in a nonviolent manner. For centuries under English law, people could not justify the use of lethal force unless they could prove that they could not preserve themselves in any other way.

Justifiable homicides in Florida tripled following the introduction of SYG in 2005.[96] In 2016, the American Medical Association's *Internal Medicine Journal* published a study showing that Florida's SYG law was associated with a 24% increase in homicides and a 32% increase in firearm-related homicides.[97] It is estimated that an additional 4,200 people were murdered with a gun in Florida in the 10-year period following enactment of SYG.[98] Texas A&M researchers have found that homicide rates in 21 states with a SYG law increased by an average of 8% over other states or 600 more homicides per year in those states alone.[99]

SYG laws have also been implemented in an inequitable manner across racial groups. John Roman of the Urban Institute analyzed data from the FBI Supplemental Homicide Reports to conduct a comparative analysis of justified homicide rates from 2005 to 2010 in SYG and non-SYG states.[100] Although racial disparities are also found in states without SYG laws, these disparities were significantly greater in SYG states. In these states, Roman found that a White shooter who killed a Black victim was 350% more likely to be found to be justified in the killing than if the same shooter killed a White victim. In SYG states, justifiable shooting rulings ranged from 3% to 15% for White-on-White, Black-on-White, and Black-on-Black killings. When the shooter was White and the victim Black, 36% were ruled justified.

Absence of National Safe Storage Laws. Each year, approximately 1,300 children die in America from a gunshot wound and close to five million children live in homes where at least one gun is loaded and unlocked. In about two out of three school shootings, the young perpetrator obtained his guns from his home or from that of a relative.[101] A recent case was the murder of 10 people and wounding of another 13 at a high school in Santa Fe, Texas. The young shooter used his father's firearms.[102] In addition to the misuse of firearms that are not stored securely, inadequate storage contributes to the theft of 300,000 guns each year.

Mark Shuster and his colleagues at the UCLA School of Medicine analyzed data from the National Health Interview Survey and found that 43% of American homes with children and firearms had at least one firearm that was not locked in a container and not locked with a trigger lock or other mechanism.[103] A more recent national survey by The Johns Hopkins Bloomberg School of Public Health found that more than half of all gun owners failed to store all their guns safely. Children under 18 were present in a third of these homes.[104]

In some countries, the safe storage of firearms—storing firearms unloaded and/or in a locked container—is a condition of gun ownership. In the US, there is an absence of national requirements relating to gun storage, and the majority of states have adopted laws enabling armed self-defense both in the home and in public places. Gun storage practices are weakening as more people are now keeping guns for self-defense and many have bought into the false narrative that guns in the home make the occupants safer.

Persistent Poverty and Disinvestment

Certain parts of America, such as the upper Midwest and parts of the Northeast (the Rust Belt), have seen industrial decline for about a half century. Cities such as Chicago, Cleveland, Pittsburgh, Detroit, and Buffalo have faced major decay and the erosion of jobs that offered a decent wage, benefits, and job security. In Chicago, a segment of the population is thriving, with a quarter of households earning over $100,000 per year. Normally, where parts of a city are booming, for every new job for an educated worker, several jobs are created for less-educated residents in the construction and service sectors. However, the racial segregation of the city has made educational and job opportunities inaccessible to large numbers of Black residents. In addition, the city has exacerbated the economic divide by investing in the downtown area rather than in poor neighborhoods.[105]

Historically, Black Americans who could afford to buy homes faced redlining, which prevented them from obtaining a federally backed loan for homes in majority-Black neighborhoods. Black people were also excluded from many White-majority neighborhoods through racially restrictive covenants. When the large factories left, so did smaller businesses that relied on customers who had worked at these factories. Alana Semuels of *The Atlantic* writes:

The North Lawndale neighborhood lost 75 percent of its businesses from 1960 to 1970 alone... Businesses weren't only leaving North Lawndale. In the South Side of Chicago, for instance, steel plants like Acme Steel and factories like the General Mills cereal plant began to close. There were 11,646 retail jobs in the Back of the Yards neighborhood on Chicago's near South Side in 1970, according to a report by the Great Cities Institute at the University of Illinois at Chicago. By 2015, there were just 1,849 such jobs.[106]

A third of Black workers in Chicago were employed in manufacturing in 1960. By 2015, just 5% of these workers were in manufacturing.

Chicago has also seen a major exodus between 2000 and 2010 of middle-class Black families who have left for better opportunities—close to 200,000 Black residents left in that decade alone. This exodus, the loss of good manufacturing jobs, and the failure of many small businesses meant that young people growing up in neighborhoods that once had a good mix of middle-class and low-income families were now surrounded by adults who were not working or who were struggling. They had fewer role models who had good jobs and who went to college.

Kenneth Graves, a resident of Chicago's South Side, states: "If you're in an environment where you see nothing but nice roses and nice people with good vibes, people living the way you're supposed to live as a citizen, then it's like a role model, you can do the same thing.... But if you're in an environment where it's crackheads and fights and arguments and gangs and poverty, it motivates you to do that as well."[107]

Three-quarters of homicides in Chicago occur among African Americans despite the fact they make up a third of the population of the city. There is a close association between concentrated poverty and homicide rates. Consider a measure called the Distressed Communities Index adopted by the Economic Innovation Group. This index rates zip codes throughout the US on seven measures: adults without a high school diploma; poverty rate; joblessness; housing vacancy rate; median income; and changes in employment and in the number of business establishments.[108]

Table 7 illustrates a strong tendency for more distressed cities to have higher homicide rates. Cities with the highest percentages of their population living in distressed neighborhoods—Detroit, Memphis, Baltimore, Philadelphia, and Chicago—also have much higher homicide rates than cities with a much lower percentage of their population living in distressed neighborhoods, such as New York and Los Angeles.

Table 7. Relationship Between Distressed Communities and Homicide Rates

CITY	POPULATION IN DISTRESSED ZIP CODES	% OF POPULATION IN DISTRESSED ZIP CODES	HOMICIDE RATE PER 100,000 IN 2018
NEW YORK, NY	1,328,870	15.9%	3.7
CHICAGO, IL	1,064,510	39.2%	20.7
HOUSTON, TX	712,140	32.8%	12.1
DETROIT, MI	688,080	98.9%	38.9
PHILADELPHIA, PA	669,990	43.3%	22.1
LOS ANGELES, CA	661,170	17.1%	5.6
PHOENIX, AZ	456,310	30.6%	8.0
MEMPHIS, TN	437,090	66.6%	28.5
SAN ANTONIO, TX	403,640	29.1%	5.6
BALTIMORE, MD	344,080	55.3%	51.0

Source: Economic Innovation Group, Distressed
Communities Index and Author's Calculations

Aside from the dearth of educational and job opportunities and, hence, the lack of social mobility in distressed areas, persistent disinvestment and concentrated poverty have been said to assault the dignity and self-worth of individuals living in these conditions. Codes of hypermasculinity follow in such environments as one's worth is measured by physical toughness and one's readiness to use violence when an affront to a person's honor occurs. Young Black men are especially susceptible to such codes as African Americans are overrepresented in distressed communities.

Social Isolation, Depression, and Disengagement of Youth

While the widespread accessibility of increasingly lethal weapons enables mass shootings, guns require human intervention to kill. The idea that in explaining gun violence one must choose between easy access to firearms and malevolent or mentally deranged individuals presents a false choice. Guns do not kill on their own. At the same time, someone bent on committing acts of violence will do far more damage with a gun than with other tools. Both the shooter and the weapon play a role in mass violence.

Some disturbing trends help explain why the US has a seemingly endless pool of individuals who, either through careful planning or impulsive actions, are prepared to annihilate several and sometimes many of their fellows.

In *Bowling Alone: The Collapse and Revival of American Communities*,[109] published in 2000, Robert Putnam of Harvard University has shown how each successive generation has been less invested in and connected to their communities. For example, as Table 8 shows, 18- to 29-year-olds were far more active in their communities in the early to mid-1970s than the same age group was in the mid-1990s.

Table 8. Civic Engagement by 18- to 29-Year-Olds

FORM OF CIVIC ENGAGEMENT	1972–1975	1996–1998
ATTENDED CHURCH WEEKLY	49%	21%
SIGNED PETITION	42%	23%
ATTENDED PUBLIC MEETING	19%	8%
WROTE CONGRESSMAN	13%	7%
COMMITTEE MEMBER OF LOCAL ORGANIZATION	13%	6%
TOOK PART IN ANY OF 12 DIFFERENT FORMS OF CIVIC LIFE	56%	31%

Source: Robert Putnam, *Bowling Alone: The Collapse and Revival of American Community*, 2000.

Teens now spend up to nine hours per day on electronic devices, social media, listening to music, or watching TV. By the time an American youth reaches 18, he or she will have spent the equivalent of two years watching television or staring at a laptop screen. They spend more than three hours alone each day.

At the same time, ties to the family, religion, country, and clubs are declining. The number of two-parent families is fewer, and the average American father spends less than 20 minutes a day in direct communication with his child.[110] Families are also in economic distress. A fifth of American families and a third of Black families had zero or negative net worth—this was the case prior to the pandemic. The majority of American families have been teetering on the edge of bankruptcy for years.[111] This situation places enormous stresses on families and such stresses can damage the mental, physical, emotional, and spiritual development of children.[112]

The Covid-19 pandemic has exacerbated the risk of youth suicide. The Centers for Disease Control and Prevention has found that a quarter of young adults (ages 18–24) have contemplated suicide during the pandemic.[113] Social isolation and fears of the virus can increase anxiety and feelings of loneliness, factors that elevate the risk of suicide. Many young people have remained at home during at least part of the pandemic and will miss out on important peer interactions and developmental milestones.

Suicide is now the second leading cause of death among young people, exceeded only by accidents.[114] Data from the Centers for Disease Control and Prevention show that the suicide rate among Americans ages 10 to 24 increased by 56% from 2007 to 2017.[115] During the same period, the rate of depression among teens rose by 63%, not a surprising trend given the link between suicide and depression. In 2017, 13% of teens reported at least one episode of depression in the past year, compared with 8% of teens in 2007, according to the National Survey on Drug Use and Health. The survey also found that, in 2017, more than one in eight Americans ages 12 to 15 experienced a major depressive episode.[116] Just 45% of teenage girls who had an episode of depression in 2019 received any treatment, and just 33% of teenage boys with depression did. In contrast, two-thirds of adults with a recent episode of depression received treatment.

A large body of research has found links between heavy technology use and poor mental health outcomes among adolescents and young adults. Dr. Jean Twenge, a psychologist at San Diego State University, notes that the use of leisure time by youth has changed dramatically. She asserts: "They spend less time with their friends in person and less time sleeping, and more time on digital media."[117] Twenge and her associates have found a steady rise in mood disorder (e.g., depression) and suicide-related outcomes between cohorts born from the early 1980s (Millennials) to the late 1990s (iGen).[118]

Black youth have shown an especially significant increase in suicide attempts since the 1990s and such attempts are the biggest predictor of death by suicide.[119] Systemic problems, such as racism, poverty, adverse childhood experiences, and disparities in mental health treatment may be driving these numbers, according to Michael Lindsey at the Silver School of Social Work, New York University. Dr. Lindsey also attributes this trend to hopelessness engendered by the way news outlets cover the African American community. By contrast, a survey of African American adolescents found that greater family and peer support, as well as community connectedness, reduced suicide risk.[120]

Chicago, a city with a large number of mass shootings in 2020, has also seen a major increase in Black suicides.[121] The deaths have been occurring overwhelmingly in neighborhoods beset with high rates of poverty and unemployment. These neighborhoods have also disproportionately borne the burden of the Covid-19 pandemic. The Centers for Disease Control and Prevention notes that anxiety and depression are up among

Black Americans as a result of the pandemic, ongoing poverty, and high-profile cases of maltreatment by the police. Stresses of this magnitude can manifest themselves in higher levels of violence, including mass shootings.

Mental Illness

Many people understandably find mass shootings to be beyond their comprehension. Their inability to comprehend such horrors often leads to the conclusion that those perpetrating these crimes are mentally ill. Surely, only a madman would massacre a group of people, sometimes total strangers, and then commit suicide! The apparent senselessness of it all leads to the conclusion that the perpetrators of these massacres are sick. The media frequently reinforce this view as it is easier to find a simplistic cause of such events than it is to offer a more complex, multi-factor explanation.

Simplistic explanations also support the media's corporate agenda, as it is more convenient to find fault with the perpetrator than to examine factors that might require society to invest more in alleviating poverty, improving education, and supporting families. The excessive reliance of cable news programs on law enforcement and security specialists, rather than criminologists or other social scientists, leads to a caricature of the offender as either sick or evil. Often, little nuance is provided of the personal, familial, community, and other factors resulting in the extreme behavior.

Indeed, some perpetrators of violence and mass shootings manifest signs of a major mental illness, such as schizophrenia or manic depressive disorder. As an example, in April 2009, J. Wong, a naturalized American from Vietnam, killed 14 people (including himself) and wounded another four in a shooting in Binghamton, New York. In the two weeks preceding the shooting, his father indicated that Wong had stopped eating dinner and became increasingly reclusive. A letter Wong sent to media outlets prior to the shooting revealed paranoid and persecutory delusions, as well as hallucinations. He blamed "undercover police" for keeping him under continuous surveillance and impeding his adjustment to American society:[122]

COP USED 24 HOURS THE TECHNiQUE OF ULTRAMODERN AND CAMERA FOR BURN THE CHEMiCAL IN MY HOUSE. FOR SWiTCH THE CHANNEL Ti.Vi. FOR ADJUST THE FAN... FROM 1990 TO 1995 NEW YORK UNDERCOVER COP TRY TO GET A CAR ACCiDENT WiTH ME. [123]

The vast majority of mass shootings do not fall in this category. At most, it has been estimated that less than 3% of violence is associated with serious mental illness.[124] Current research indicates that there is a minimal relationship between psychiatric disorders and violence when substance abuse is absent.[125] Thus, the assumption that individuals with mental illness are at "high risk" to commit violence generally and gun violence in particular is not supported by the evidence. It has been estimated that a person is 15 times more likely to be struck by lightning in a given year than to be killed by a stranger who has been diagnosed with schizophrenia or chronic psychosis.[126]

Paul Applebaum, a Columbia University psychiatrist, notes that even if all violence by those with serious mental illnesses could be prevented, well over 90% of violence would remain.[127] The mentally ill are much more likely to be victims of crime or to commit suicide than to be perpetrators of violence. Applebaum adds that when people with mental disorders like schizophrenia commit violent acts, it is often some other factor, such as substance abuse, that is more influential than the disorder itself.

Mass shooters only rarely have had verified histories of being in treatment for serious mental illness. A far larger group of shooters are individuals who often feel aggrieved, are extremely angry, and fantasize about violent revenge.

Psychiatrists James Knoll and George Annas identify several types of resentful mass murderers.[128]

The *school-resentful* type targets schoolmates and is motivated by hostile revenge. These individuals have often been bullied or are socially alienated and feel rejected and humiliated by their peers. The Virginia Tech and Columbine shooters fall in this category.

The *workplace-resentful* type is the aggrieved former or current employee who is angry with a supervisor, colleagues, or some other aspect of the work environment and commits murder in the workplace. They are often depressed, externalize blame onto others, and obsess about their feelings of being wronged. An example was D. Craddock, an engineer at Virginia Beach's public utilities department. On May 31, 2019, he submitted his resignation by email and then showed up armed at his workplace, killing 12 people and injuring four others. In the days leading up to the shooting, he was said to have had some physical scuffles with co-workers and was threatened with disciplinary action.[129]

The *indiscriminate-resentful* type is full of rage, depressed, and often paranoid. He lashes out in some public place and the victims are often chosen randomly. An example is J. Huberty, who murdered 22 and injured another 19 in a San Diego McDonald's restaurant in 1984. He told his wife just prior to the offense that "society had their chance" and that he was heading out to go "hunting humans."[130]

J. Reid Meloy, a forensic psychologist, states that many mass shooters display some paranoid thinking, though most are not deeply ill. Rather, they are "injustice collectors" who are prone to perceive insults and failures as cumulative and tend to blame a person or group for their problems.

If you have this paranoid streak, this vigilance, this sense that others have been persecuting you for years, there's an accumulation of maltreatment and an intense urge to stop that persecution.... That may never happen. The person may never act on the urge. But when they do, typically there's a triggering event. It's a loss in love or work—something that starts a clock ticking, that starts the planning.[131]

Another indication that mental illness does not play a critical role in explaining the vast majority of mass shootings in the US is the fact that, while the US is an outlier in its number of mass shootings when compared with other countries, the rates of mental illness are in line with other countries.[132]

Contagion and the Media's Role

Contagion is the notion that one mass shooting might stimulate others to commit more of the same. This phenomenon has been documented across a variety of behaviors, from airline hijackings and smoking cessation to binge eating and suicide.[133] One study showed that from 1968 to 1972 successful hijackings of civilian aircraft "generated" additional hijacking attempts of the same type (either transportation or extortion).[134] The appearance of suicide clusters in high schools[135] and the success of efforts to prevent suicides by curbing media coverage of public suicides indicate the role of contagion in suicide.[136]

Researcher Todd Miller and his associates found that the homicide rate increases following high-profile boxing matches.[137] In the case of mass shootings, a contagion effect would be said to exist if a single mass shooting incident increased the likelihood of other mass shootings in the near future. Evidence now exists that when a mass shooting occurs, there is a temporary increase in the probability of another event within approximately 13 days.[138]

Contagion does not explain the underlying "causes" of mass shootings as much as it does the spread of these events. Why might a mass shooting spawn others? The process of imitation may be useful in answering this question as generalized imitation is the learned ability to perform behaviors that are similar to behaviors observed or described, even when performance is delayed. This skill is acquired at an early age and gradually strengthened through many life experiences.

James Meindl of the University of Memphis notes that people are more likely to imitate someone similar to themselves, especially in age and gender, and one who is seen to be competent and to be rewarded for his or her behavior.[139] Such rewards can include elevated social status. When perpetrators imitate other mass shooters, they are usually observing such events through media sources, and research has shown that media can influence imitation.

Some shooters, such as the Sutherland Springs, Texas, church shooter, have been found to have an obsession with mass shootings or their perpetrators.[140] The young man who committed the atrocity at Sandy Hook Elementary School in Newtown, Connecticut had studied the Columbine massacre as well as others.[141] The individual who shot over 100 people at the Pulse nightclub in Orlando, Florida had studied a previous attack in San Bernardino, California, which was also inspired by a radical Islamic ideology. The White nationalist who murdered 23 people in El Paso, Texas had seen the video posted by the man who had committed the mosque massacres in Christchurch, New Zealand.

Saturated media coverage often follows high-casualty mass shootings. This coverage tends to repeatedly describe the event in detail, weapons used, the shooter, his ideology (where relevant), and his life story. This detailed coverage can directly influence imitation. The shooter achieves social status through the notoriety gained from the numerous news reports. Images displaying shooters aiming or brandishing guns at the camera project danger and toughness. Individuals may identify with the life story of perpetrators. Repeated reports of body counts reward the act by underscoring the competence of the shooter.

The large number of shootings in America over the last few years gives prospective shooters almost an unlimited number of shooters and shootings to emulate, thereby contributing to even more mass shootings. For example, on July 5, 2020, 15 mass shootings occurred in just one day.[142] For those living in Chicago, Baltimore, Saint Louis, or some other place experiencing multiple mass shootings a year, there are numerous local shootings to emulate.

The Covid-19 Pandemic's Impact on Violence

The previous chapter showed that the pandemic, as well as the response to it, was associated with a dramatic increase in mass shootings in the US in the summer of 2020. Richard Rosenfeld and Ernesto Lopez of the University of Missouri showed that homicide rates from June through August increased by 53% from 2019 to 2020.[143] At the same time, many other violent crimes (e.g., domestic assault, robbery) showed no significant increases, and residential burglary was down by about 25% in the summer of 2020 from the same time in 2019. This last finding is easy to understand as people spent far more time at home in 2020 and those breaking into homes usually prefer not to encounter the occupants.

A number of factors may explain the increase in mass shootings and homicides. The pandemic has increased poverty, unemployment, hunger, and housing insecurity. The economic downturn resulting from the shutdowns associated with the pandemic increased levels of hopelessness, especially among young people of color. The pandemic-related lockdowns have also frustrated young people hoping to socialize with their peers. In addition, the anti-violence efforts of street outreach workers have been impeded by the pandemic. *New York Times* reporters Emily Badger and Quoctrung Bui write:

The pandemic has frayed all kinds of institutions and infrastructure that hold communities together, that watch over streets, that mediate conflicts, that simply give young people something to do. Schools, libraries, recreation centers and public pools have closed. Nonprofits, churches and sports leagues have scaled back. Mentors, social workers and counselors have been hampered by social distancing. And programs devised to reduce gun violence—and that have proved effective in studies—have been upended by the pandemic. Summer jobs programs were cut this year. Violence intervention workers were barred from hospitals. Group behavioral therapy programs meant to be intimate and in-person have moved, often haltingly, online.[144]

Consider Chicago's READI program for men at highest risk of gun violence. The program offers transitional jobs, cognitive behavioral therapy, and other support. The jobs evaporated with the pandemic—this was replaced by payments from the program—and online therapy was beset with some major obstacles. Those running the program were aware that if these individuals lose their safety net, they would engage in criminal activity.[145]

Two examples from Canada illustrate the stress and violence that may arise as a result of the pandemic and associated lockdowns. In Ottawa, C. Hurren, armed with loaded guns, was arrested after a pickup truck crashed through the residence of Prime Minister Justin Trudeau. Hurren left a note saying Covid was ruining him financially and restrictions were turning Canada into a communist dictatorship.[146] The pandemic may also have triggered Canada's worst mass killing in April 2020. G. Wortman was said by a friend to be "paranoid about the pandemic." He liquidated his investments and stockpiled food and fuel shortly before he murdered 22 people in the province of Nova Scotia.

Racial Tensions and Reckoning

In the summer of 2020, a number of high-profile killings of Black persons by the police galvanized a movement, including many protests, calling for police accountability and racial justice. While these protests were largely nonviolent,[147] together with the end of pandemic-related lockdowns, they were followed by acts of violence reflecting widespread hopelessness, despair, and anger in the Black community. Criminologist Rosenfeld indicates that we have observed spikes in violence in American cities in the past following racial unrest. For example, an increase in violence was observed following the 2014 police-involved killing of Michael Brown and subsequent unrest in Ferguson, Missouri—referred to as the "Ferguson effect."

Rosenfeld explains this phenomenon by pointing to the deterioration of police legitimacy during periods of racial unrest, even where relations between police and the community are already strained.[148] He argues that when confidence in law enforcement drops, there is an increase in street justice, meaning that people are more likely to resolve disputes through violence rather than relying on the police. Also, chronic citizen discontent may boil over into violence when triggered by questionable uses of force by police. In addition, police departments may be less effective in keeping the peace during periods of unrest as morale may suffer when they are under closer scrutiny and being criticized for civilian deaths and questionable tactics.

Kansas City is an example of a city with a major increase in homicide in 2020.[149] Many murders followed petty arguments that escalated. Law enforcement officials have attributed these incidents to restlessness and anger. They found that 30 of the homicides in 2020 were due to arguments, some involving individuals without a serious criminal history. Economic hardship appeared to be a factor in some of the killings and just 15 were deemed to be drug-related. In nearly 50 cases, the police could not identify a clear motive.

Community leaders in the predominantly Black East Side of Kansas City have observed that there was an added sense of despair in 2020. The Reverend Darren Faulkner, who runs a local anti-violence program, said the latest wave of police killings of Black people left many of his clients with a profound sense of hopelessness and feeling that they will never thrive in the present system.

People have gotten to the point where they just don't give a damn. I don't care about me. I certainly don't care about you.

And so I can go shoot your house or shoot you right on the spot because you talked to me crazy, you looked at me crazy. I'm sure the lockdown didn't help. When you already have a stressed economic situation and you put a lot of folks out of work, and a lot of teenagers out of school, it's a volatile situation.[150]

Routine Activities and Mass Shootings

Emergency isolation orders, border closures, social distancing, mask wearing, and mandated lockdowns are inconvenient and costly, but it is hoped that it will at least test theories as to why crime really happens. Criminologist Marcus Felson states:

The 'stay-at-home' mandates brought about the most wide-reaching, significant, and sudden alteration of the lives of billions of people in human history.... Practically overnight, the entire country ceased or significantly reduced day-to-day travels, eliminating commutes from home to work, as well as leisure activities, shopping trips, social gatherings, the ability to dine out, and more...a positive byproduct of these unprecedented events is a dramatic drop in crime rates.[151]

The changes in crime have been uneven and dependent on the type of crime. However, these changes illustrate how the routine activities of the population can shape crime. John Roman, a researcher with the University of Chicago, provides the following "routine activities" explanation for the spike in homicide in the summer of 2020. Routine activities theory posits that crime requires a motivated offender, a suitable target, and an absence of guardianship (protection) in relation to that target.

Young men are stuck at home instead of working or going to school. They are experiencing the same anxiety the rest of us are experiencing, but in neighborhoods with a long history of violence they have the added burden of accumulated traumas, including unresolved disputes. And critically, the people they have serious beefs with are also stuck at home and close by. Imagine someone you loved was killed or shot or beaten and you know (or you think you know) who did it (that is the motivation). You are stuck at home without access to supports, a caring teacher, work for a sense of purpose, or professional supports (that is the lack of guardianship). And the guy who did it is just a few streets away (that's the target). It's just a toxic situation.

Now add to the mix easy access to guns. The number of guns purchased since the beginning of the pandemic is astronomical.... These guns leak into to the illegal market and become crime guns. Some are bought for this purpose, but many more are stolen from homes and cars.[152]

Social Factors vs. Gun Availability: A False Choice

America accounts for a third of the world's mass shootings and stands alone when it is compared with other high-income countries. As we have seen, mental illness does not account for this situation as most mass shootings are not committed by the mentally ill and the US does not have higher rates of serious mental illness than comparable countries. For example, the prevalence of schizophrenia in the US is lower than in most countries.[153] The notion that violent media and video games are responsible for America's status as a world leader in mass shootings is also not supported by facts. Video game spending per capita is much higher in countries like Japan, South Korea, and the Netherlands, countries with a fraction of the gun violence found in the US.[154]

The evidence presented in this chapter has shown that easy access to guns in America, including weapons originally designed for the military, and weak gun laws are important factors driving gun violence and mass shootings. In addition, declining community engagement by youth, increasing levels of youth depression, and economic factors, as well as the impact of the Covid-19 pandemic and racial unrest, have all contributed to the current explosion in mass shootings.

Imitation, too, can foster the spread of these events in the US as one shooter emulates those who have come before. It is a false choice to say that gun violence and mass shootings are either due to weak gun laws or social factors, such as youth alienation, racism, and depression. Social factors explain why some people are motivated to commit violence and guns provide the means to commit mass shootings.

Those objecting to more gun regulation claim that America has more gun violence because it is a more crime-ridden and violent society than other affluent countries and not because there are more guns in America. The higher levels of homicide, they say, are because of a culture that is more violent than in comparable countries. As indicated at the outset of this chapter, this view has been discredited by legal scholars Franklin Zimring and the late Gordon Hawkins, who showed that the US, when compared with other developed countries, does not stand out with respect to property crimes and most forms of violence.[155] America does, however, stand out in its level of lethal violence. Zimring and Hawkins consider the high levels of gun ownership in the US as the most important factor driving America's exceptionally high rate of lethal violence.

Adam Lankford of the University of Alabama has found that a country's rate of gun ownership is correlated positively with the odds it would experience a mass shooting, meaning that higher ownership levels are associated with more mass shootings.[156] This correlation held when he controlled for homicide rates, suggesting that mass shootings were better explained by a society's access to guns than by its baseline level of violence. As indicated at the outset of this chapter, evidence at the state level shows that mass shootings tend to be more common in states with higher gun ownership levels and more permissive gun laws. Globally, evidence from 130 studies in 10 countries suggests that the simultaneous implementation of laws imposing multiple firearms restrictions is associated with reductions in firearm deaths.[157]

Thus, while a number of societal factors create the conditions predisposing some people to commit mass shootings and other acts of gun violence, high gun ownership levels and weak gun laws in most of the US furnish the means through which these individuals can produce the carnage we have seen.

5
Mass Shootings in America—2019 and 2020

This chapter presents the findings from this writer's analysis of mass shootings occurring in America in 2019 and 2020. Some of the findings are likely to surprise the reader. In part, our expectations have been formed by the media's coverage of mass shootings, and the media tend to cover the most extreme incidents. A study of gun assaults in Philadelphia, Cincinnati, and Rochester (New York) found that shooting incidents not involving fatalities were less likely to be covered. Shootings involving Black and male victims were also underreported.[158] Another study showed that more coverage was extended to shootings in which the assailant was believed to have a mental illness and those targeting schools, government buildings, or houses of worship.[159]

As indicated in Chapter 2, this study defines a mass shooting as an incident in which four or more people are shot (not necessarily killed), excluding the shooter. That chapter also explains the justification for this definition, as well as the reasons for the selection of the Gun Violence Archive as the source identifying the shootings that occurred in 2019 and 2020. As explained in Chapter 2, the GVA's definition of mass shooting includes nonfatal shootings of four or more people and includes incidents committed in private settings as well as those that are domestic and gang-related. The GVA was also selected as the source for this study due to its thoroughness and professionalism in ensuring it has captured virtually every mass shooting in America.

Tables 5 and 6 in Chapter 3 showed that mass shootings increased steadily from 2014 to 2019 and exploded in 2020 due to the pandemic, the associated economic calamity, and racial unrest stemming from police killings of a number of Black citizens.

Mass Shootings in 2019–2020

Table 9 shows that the 1,029 mass shootings uncovered by the Gun Violence Archive (GVA) in 2019–2020 resulted in nearly 1,000 deaths and a total of over 5,000 casualties. The GVA considers a mass shooting as an incident in which four or more people are shot and/or killed in a single event, not including the perpetrator. As this is a minimum requirement, casualties often exceed this threshold. In the two-year period covered by this study, shootings produced up to 46 people shot—the Walmart shooting in El Paso, Texas. On average, across all shootings in 2019–2020, one person was killed and about four were injured in these shootings. While high-casualty shootings like the one in El Paso receive a great deal of media attention, many of those with four or five casualties receive modest coverage, often in local media only.

Table 9. Number of People Killed and Injured in Mass Shootings, 2019–2020 (1,029 cases)

	KILLED	INJURED	CASUALTIES
TOTAL	923	4,226	5,149
AVERAGE PER INCIDENT	.9	4.1	5.0

Source: Gun Violence Archive

Mass Shootings by Region, State, City, and Community Size

The American South accounted for 460 mass shootings, nearly half of all incidents in the country in 2019–2020 (Table 10). Another quarter occurred in the Midwest. Both of these regions experienced a disproportionate number of mass shootings in relation to their population. By contrast, the West and Northeast each accounted for less than 15% of the mass shootings in the US, a lower percentage than what one would expect by reference to their population.

Historically, the South has been the region with the highest homicide rate in the country.[160] Poverty, cultural factors, and a history of racial injustice and occupational segregation have all played a significant role.[161] In the Midwest, cities like Chicago, St. Louis, Detroit, and Cleveland have seen a major downturn in manufacturing, resulting in the decline of working-class neighborhoods. Suburban flight and the concentration of the impoverished in housing projects further exacerbated this decline. Chapter 4 discussed the concentration of poverty in Chicago in certain African American neighborhoods and its contribution to violence and criminality therein. Data presented in that chapter show the link between urban distress and homicide.

Table 10. Mass Shootings by US Region, 2019–2020

REGION	% OF US POPULATION	# OF MASS SHOOTINGS	% OF US MASS SHOOTINGS
NORTHEAST	17.1	146	14.2
SOUTH	38.3	460	44.7
MIDWEST	20.8	276	26.8
WEST	23.9	147	14.3

Source: Gun Violence Archive. Population estimates
by region were derived from the US Census.

Table 11 lists the 10 states with the highest and lowest number of mass shootings in 2019–2020. Illinois had the largest number of mass shootings with 111, followed by California with 85. Four states—Vermont, Rhode Island, New Hampshire, and North Dakota—did not have any mass shootings in the two-year period covered by this study. When state population differences are taken into account, Louisiana has the highest rate of mass shootings per million people, followed by Illinois, Maryland, and Missouri. Each of these four states has a city with a large number of mass shootings—New Orleans, Chicago, Baltimore, and St. Louis—which accounts for the state's high rate of these shootings.

The table also displays the relationship between mass shootings, state gun laws, and state household gun ownership levels. The 10 states listed with the largest number of mass shootings tended to have a higher ranking on gun laws, meaning that their laws overall were stricter than the 10 states with the fewest mass shootings. The states with the largest number of mass shootings also tended to have fewer households with guns than the states with the fewest mass shootings. Thus, contrary to previous studies, states with the largest number of mass shootings overall had stronger gun laws and lower levels of gun ownership than states with the fewest mass shootings. This finding suggests that factors other than gun laws and ownership levels have an impact on mass shootings. Previous studies that found stricter gun laws and lower gun ownership levels to be associated with fewer mass shootings adjusted for economic and social factors influencing mass shootings, thereby isolating the effect of gun laws and household ownership.[162]

One explanation for the finding here is that states with the highest number of mass shootings have a larger urban population and states with the lowest number of these incidents have more of a rural character. This is shown in the final column. Thus, comparing more urban with more rural states without adjusting for this difference makes it difficult to draw conclusions about the role of gun laws and gun ownership, as other critical factors impacting mass shootings have not been taken into account. This said, on the face of it, we can conclude that factors other than gun laws and ownership levels, such as economic distress and degree of urbanization, play an important role in mass shootings.

It is also likely that more urban states with higher gun homicide rates have passed stricter gun laws in response to their higher levels of violence. Thus, the relationship between gun laws and violence works both ways. Apart from gun laws having an effect on violence, more violence leads to the adoption of tougher gun laws. Stricter state gun laws may also not be associated with low gun violence rates because bordering states may have more lax laws, allowing prohibited purchasers to obtain guns from neighboring states. The many guns used in crime in Chicago that are purchased in Indiana is a case in point. The patchwork of gun laws throughout the US makes a compelling case for some national laws.

Table 11. States with Most and Fewest Mass Shootings, Ranking on Gun Laws and Household Gun Ownership

RANK	STATE	# OF MASS SHOOTINGS IN 2019–2020	RATE PER MIL-LION	RANK ON GUN LAWS	% HOMES WITH GUNS	% URBAN
1	Illinois	111	8.76	8	27.8	88.5
2	California	85	2.15	1	28.3	95.0
3	Texas	65	2.24	34	45.7	84.7
4	Louisiana	53	11.40	32	53.1	73.2
5	Pennsyl-vania	52	4.06	12	40.7	78.7
6	Florida	50	2.33	22	35.3	91.2
7	New York	48	2.47	4	19.9	87.9
8	Missouri	40	6.52	46	48.8	70.4
9	Maryland	40	6.62	6	30.2	87.2
10	Ohio	39	3.34	24	40.0	77.9
AVERAGE			5.0	18.9	37.0	83.5
41	Maine	1	.74	34	46.8	38.7
42	South Dakota	1	1.13	44	55.3	56.7
43	W. Virginia	1	.56	34	58.5	48.7
44	Wyoming	1	1.73	48	66.2	64.8
45	Utah	1	.31	27	46.8	90.6
46	Idaho	1	.56	48	60.1	70.6
47	Rhode Island	0	0	9	14.8	90.7
48	Vermont	0	0	23	50.5	38.9
49	New Hamp.	0	0	30	41.1	60.3
50	North Dakota	0	0	35	55.1	59.9
AVERAGE			.50	33.2	49.5	61.9

Sources: Giffords Law Center state scorecard; T. Schell et al, State-level estimates of household firearm ownership, Rand Corporation, 2020. State urbanization data were drawn from the Iowa Community Indicators Program, Iowa State University.

Table 12 lists the cities with the largest number of mass shootings in 2019–2020. Collectively, these 13 cities account for 30.9% or almost a third of all mass shootings in the US. Chicago led the way with 84, a rate of almost one a week over the two-year period. On two occasions during July 2020, the city experienced two mass shootings in a single day. The city with the next highest total was Philadelphia, with 43 mass shootings during the study period. However, these cities did not lead when the population of these cities was taken into account. St. Louis had the highest rate of mass shootings per million people, followed by Baltimore, New Orleans, Chicago, and Atlanta.

Table 12. Cities with the Largest Number of Mass Shootings, 2019–2020

RANK	CITY	# OF MASS SHOOTINGS	RATE PER MILLION
1	Chicago	84	31.0
2	Philadelphia	43	27.1
3	Baltimore	28	46.5
4	New York (all boroughs)	27	3.2
5	St. Louis	24	79.3
6	Houston	20	8.6
7	New Orleans	17	43.5
8	Atlanta	15	30.1
9	Washington	14	20.5
10	Detroit	13	19.3
10	Memphis	13	20.0
12	Los Angeles	10	2.5
12	Cleveland	10	26.0

Sources: Gun Violence Archive and author's calculations.

A 10% sample of mass shootings during the study period reveals that, while most occur in the largest cities, communities of all sizes are vulnerable (Table 13). About a third occurred in cities with a population of more than a half million, while a quarter took place in cities with a population between 10,001 and 100,000 and in cities with a population between 100,001–500,000. Just over 10% occurred in communities of less than 10,000 people.

Table 13. Mass Shootings and Community Size, 2019–2020

COMMUNITY POPULATION	# OF MASS SHOOTINGS (10% SAMPLE)	% OF MASS SHOOTINGS
LESS THAN 10,000	13	12.6
10,001–100,000	25	24.2
100,001–500,000	29	28.2
500,001 AND OVER	36	35.0
TOTAL	103	

Source: Gun Violence Archive

The Victims

Table 14 displays the gender of mass shooting victims. In a third of the cases in which the gender of all victims was known, all the victims were males. All the victims were females in just 1.6% of the cases. In about two-thirds of the cases where information on gender was available, a combination of male and female victims was shot. It is clear that males are more likely to be targeted in mass shootings as just a dozen shootings involved female victims only. The fact that so many cases involve female as well as male victims suggests recklessness on the part of shooters who most often target or are involved in some form of dispute with another male. It appears that, other than in domestic disputes, women tend to be bystanders caught up in a shooting that involves two or more males.

Table 14. The Gender of Victims in Mass Shootings, 2019 and 2020

TOTAL CASES	BOTH MALES & FEMALES	MALES ONLY	FEMALES ONLY	INCOMPLETE INFORMATION
1,029	484	250	12	283

Source: Gun Violence Archive

In 2019–2020, mass shootings in the US victimized a number of infants, including one as young as one month and, in a drive-by shooting in Louisiana, a pregnant mother was shot in the womb, ending her pregnancy. The oldest victim of a mass shooting was 93. Table 15 shows that when we examine those cases where all the victims' ages are known, the average age of the youngest victim was 18.7 and the average age of the oldest victim was 38.2. Children under 18 years of age were shot or killed in more than a third of the cases. A study cited in *Newsweek* revealed that the average mass shooting in 2019 occurred .4 miles from a school and .7 miles from a place of interest for children (park, playground, rec center), illustrating the exposure to violence of kids.[163] While those under 18 were sometimes targeted, the frequent victimization of young children, as well as the elderly, suggests an indifference on the part of many shooters to the possibility of shooting innocent bystanders.

Table 15. Age of Victims in Mass Shootings, 2019 and 2020

NUMBER OF CASES IN WHICH ALL VICTIMS' AGES WERE KNOWN	AVERAGE AGE OF YOUNGEST VICTIM	AVERAGE AGE OF OLDEST VICTIM	CASES IN WHICH CHILDREN AND TEENS <18 YEARS SHOT
448	18.7	38.2	165 (36.8%)

Source: Gun Violence Archive

Table 16 displays the cases in which law enforcement officers were known to have been shot. In most of these cases, the type of firearm used was unknown. In two cases, both an assault-style rifle and a handgun were used. In half the cases in which the firearm used was known, an assault rifle or a pistol with tactical gear were the weapons chosen. While the number of cases here is small, this finding supports growing evidence that assault weapons pose a direct threat to police officers.[164]

Table 16. Law Enforcement Officers Shot in Mass Shootings and Firearms Used, 2019 and 2020

TOTAL CASES	CASES IN WHICH POLICE OFFICERS WERE SHOT	MILITARY-STYLE RIFLES & PISTOLS	OTHER HANDGUNS	FIREARM TYPE UNKNOWN
1,029	22	4	4	16

Source: Gun Violence Archive

The Suspects

In over nine in 10 (93.2%) of the 1,028 mass shootings in 2019–2020 where information was available on their fate, suspects left the scene unharmed (Table 17). Of those hurt at the scene and where sufficient information was available to ascertain the cause of death, a suicide was the most likely cause (29 cases). Often this was a murder-suicide in the case of a family shooting. Suspects were shot by police or security personnel in 15 cases. Shooters were shot by victims in 10 (fewer than 1%) of the cases in which sufficient information was available on the cause of death, and one of these cases involved a dispute rather than a clear aggressor. This finding supports previous research indicating that the successful use of guns by civilians to thwart aggressors is rare. This said, the successful use of a gun to prevent a mass shooting altogether would not have been captured by this study. It is clear, however, that the use of guns by civilian victims to put an end to a mass shooting is a rare event.

Table 17. Injuries/Fatalities Sustained by Suspects, 2019–2020

# OF CASES	SUSPECT NOT HARMED	SUICIDE OF SUSPECT	SUSPECT SHOT BY POLICE/ SECURITY PERSONNEL	SUSPECT SHOT BY VICTIM/ DEFENSIVE GUN USE	INSUFFICIENT INFORMATION ON CAUSE OF INJURY/DEAT H
1,028*	958	29	15	10	16

*Cases in which information was available on the fate of the suspect(s)

Table 18 shows that where the gender of mass shooting suspects was known, shooters were overwhelmingly men (95.9% of the cases). In just two of 392 cases (.5%) in which the gender of suspects was known, the shooters were women only. In another 14 cases (3.6%), the shooters were a combination of males and females. In seven in 10 cases in which males were the shooters, they operated alone. The average age of suspects was 27. However, 41 of 190 shooters (21.6%) in 2020 where the shooter's age was known were under 21.

Table 18. The Gender and Number of Mass Shooting Suspects, 2019 and 2020

CASES WHERE SUSPECTS' GENDER WAS KNOWN	ONE MALE	TWO OR MORE MALES	FEMALES ONLY	BOTH MALES AND FEMALES
392	263	113	2	14

Source: Gun Violence Archive

The Weapons

Assault weapons figured prominently in the mass shootings (Table 19). Handguns were used in over half the mass shootings. This is not surprising as handguns account for most guns used in crime.[165] Assault-style rifles were used in at least a third of all the mass shootings in 2019–2020. They figure even more prominently if some of the unspecified types of rifles (Column #4) were, in fact, assault rifles.

Table 19. Weapons Used in Mass Shootings, 2019 and 2020

CASES WITH INFORM-ATION ON FIREARMS USED	ASSAULT-STYLE RIFLE	HANDGUN	RIFLE (UNSPECIFIED)**	SHOTGUN
132*	46	81	17 (including 3 long rifles)	6

Source: Gun Violence Archive

*Numbers in the row exceed 132 as some suspects used more than one type of firearm

**Some rifles may also have been assault rifles; however, no information was provided as to the specific type of rifle

Table 20 illustrates the vital role of assault-style weapons in mass shootings. FBI data show that, in 2018, when the type of firearm used was known, rifles were used in just 4.1% of all murders in the US.[166] However, rifles, most of which were assault rifles, were used in 47.7% of the mass shootings in 2019–2020. Thus, assault and other rifles were about 12 times as likely to be used in mass shootings than in murders overall (47.7% vs. 4.1%), a clear indication that these weapons are often the weapons of choice and enable mass shootings.

Table 20. Frequency of Rifles Used in Mass Shootings vs. Murders Overall

	MASS SHOOTINGS (2019–2020)	MURDER OVERALL (2018)
CASES IN WHICH RIFLES WERE USED	63	297
CASES IN WHICH FIREARMS USED AND TYPE IS KNOWN	132	7,302
% OF CASES IN WHICH RIFLES WERE USED	47.7%	4.1%

Sources: Gun Violence Archive and FBI, 2018 Crime in the United States.

Race and Mass Shootings

The African American community experiences a disproportionate number of mass shootings. In this study, demographic data were obtained for each zip code in which a shooting occurred. For shootings occurring in alternate months of 2020 (January, March, May, July, September, and November), we identified the dominant racial group in the community in which a shooting occurred, where the precise location (address) of the incident was available. Table 21 shows that in the 127 cases that met the criteria, close to three in five incidents occurred in a zip code that had a majority or plurality White (including Hispanic) population. Close to 40% of the mass shootings occurred in an area with a majority or plurality Black population. By comparison, Black Americans make up just 13% of the country's population. A study using census tracts rather than zip codes to determine the demographics of neighborhoods in which shootings occurred found that nearly 50% of the shootings took place in Black-majority neighborhoods.[167]

Our source, the Gun Violence Archive, does not provide the race of suspects or victims. Determination of the race of the parties on the basis of neighborhood demographics, whether through the use of zip code or census tract information, is necessarily imprecise as suspects of one race may commit their offenses in neighborhoods inhabited primarily by members of another race. Based on photographs of mass shooting victims, this writer's impression—albeit a highly subjective one—is that Table 21 underestimates the percentage of mass shooting victims who are Black.

Table 21. Racial Composition of Communities and Mass Shootings, 2020

DOMINANT GROUP IN ZIP CODE OF MASS SHOOTING	NUMBER OF CASES*	% OF CASES
WHITE (INCLUDING HISPANIC)	76	59.8
BLACK	50	39.4
ASIAN	1	.8
TOTAL CASES	127	100.0

Source: Gun Violence Archive and zipdatamaps.com

*The figures are based on a 50% sample of mass shootings in 2020

High-Casualty Mass Shootings

Table 22 displays the 31 high-casualty incidents during 2019–2020. In this study, a high-casualty mass shooting was one in which six or more people, excluding the shooter, were killed or in which a total of 10 or more people were shot but not necessarily killed. On average, close to 15 people were shot in these incidents. In six of these incidents, seven or more victims were killed. The period from July 28, 2019 to August 31, 2019 saw four especially deadly shootings: the Gilroy (California) Garlic Festival shooting; the Walmart shooting in El Paso (Texas); the Dayton (Ohio) Oregon District shooting; and the Odessa (Texas) shooting spree. Assault-style weapons were used in each of these shootings.

Where the type of weapon used was known and disclosed, it is evident that assault-style rifles or handguns equipped with tactical gear (laser aiming devices, silencers) were well represented in these high-casualty mass shootings. In 11 cases in which the weapon type was available, assault-style rifles were used in more than half (six cases) and handguns with tactical devices were used in two more incidents. This is noteworthy as rifles of any kind are used in just 4% of all murders.[168]

The analysis of high-casualty incidents in 2019–2020 does not support the notion that many of the worst mass shootings are family-related, are terror-related, or occur in schools. There was one family-related and one terror-related incident among these shootings and no high-casualty school shootings during the two-year period. In addition, in only one case was there an explicit reference to the possibility that the shooter suffered from a serious mental illness. Two of these incidents occurred in the workplace and a third shooting occurred after the shooter was fired from his job. However, the circumstances most often found among these cases involved some form of dispute; specifically, gang or group-related conflicts, spontaneous disputes that did not appear to be group-related, or disputes originating or playing out inside or in the vicinity of a bar or nightclub.

Table 22. High-Casualty Mass Shootings (6+ victims killed and/or 10+ shot), 2019–2020

LOCATION	DATE	CASUAL-TIES	CIRCUMSTANCES	WEAPONS
AURORA, IL	February 15, 2019	5 killed, 6 injured	Fired employee shoots employees at a plant	Handgun with laser aiming device
VIRGINIA BEACH, VA	May 31, 2019	12 killed, 4 injured	Employee resigned, shot employees, others at workplace	Handguns, a tactical gun with a silencer
ALLENTOWN, PA	June 20, 2019	0 killed, 10 injured	Gang-related shooting outside club	
SOUTH BEND, IN	June 23, 2019	1 killed, 10 injured	Bar shooting	
BROOKLYN, NY	July 27, 2019	1 killed, 11 injured	Gang-related dispute and shootout at party	
GILROY, CA	July 28, 2019	3 killed, 17 injured	Racially motivated shooting at a garlic festival	AK-47 assault weapon, 75-round magazine
EL PASO, TX	August 3, 2019	23 killed, 23 injured	Walmart shooting motivated by hatred of Mexicans	AK-47 assault weapon
DAYTON, OH	August 4, 2019	9 killed, 17 injured	Shooting in entertainment district—mental illness, drugs may have played a role	AR-15 assault weapon
ODESSA, TX	August 31, 2019	7 killed, 23 injured	Shooting spree suspect shooting people from car	AM-15 assault weapon
LANCASTER, SC	September 21, 2019	2 killed, 8 injured	Shooting inside and outside a bar; part of ongoing dispute	

FRESNO, CA	November 17, 2019	4 killed, 6 injured	Retaliatory gang shooting at a house party	
NEW ORLEANS, LA	December 1, 2019	0 killed, 12 injured	Dispute and shootout involving two people; bystanders shot	
PENSACOLA, FL	December 6, 2019	3 killed, 8 injured	Terrorist attack at naval station	
CHICAGO, IL	December 22, 2019	0 killed, 12 injured	Dispute and shootout at a house party	Handgun
KANSAS CITY, MO	January 19, 2020	1 killed, 15 injured	Individual shoots at clubgoers after being denied entry	
CLEVELAND, OH	March 7, 2020	1 killed, 18 injured	Shootout among biker groups at a house party	
MONCURE, NC	March 15, 2020	6 killed, 0 injured	Murder of family and others followed by suicide	
BOGALUSA, LA	May 16, 2020	0 killed, 13 injured	Drug-related shooting at a vigil for a homicide victim	
VALHERMOSO SPRINGS, AL	June 4, 2020	7 killed, 0 injured	Murder following a dispute among club members	
MINNEAPOLIS, MN	June 21, 2020	0 killed, 11 injured	Shooting outside of a restaurant during racial justice protests	
ATLANTA, GA	July 5, 2020	2 killed, 12 injured	Dispute during a large July 4 gathering	
GREENVILLE, SC	July 5, 2020	2 killed, 8 injured	Gang-related dispute in a nightclub leading to a shooting	
PEORIA, IL	July 19, 2020	0 killed, 13 injured	Dispute at a large gathering; many bystanders shot	
CHICAGO, IL	July 21, 2020	0 killed,15 injured	Gang-related drive-by shooting and shootout at a funeral	
WASHINGTON, DC	August 9, 2020	1 killed, 21 injured	Shooting by four individuals at a large gathering	Handguns

CINCINNATI, OH	August 16, 2020	2 killed, 9 injured	Insufficient information on shooting	
AGUANGA, CA	September 7, 2020	7 killed, 0 injured	Shootout at illegal marijuana growing operation	
ROCHESTER, NY	September 19, 2020	2 killed, 14 injured	Argument and shootout at a large house party	Handguns
GREENWOOD, MS	October 24, 2020	2 killed, 8 injured	Gathering after a funeral in a house	AR-15
AIKEN, SC	November 28, 2020	1 killed, 10 injured	Drive-by shooting outside nightclub	AR-15, handgun
GRENADA, MS	November 29, 2020	0 killed, 11 injured	Shootout at biker club	
AVERAGE # OF CASUALTIES		3.4 killed and 11.2 injured		

Source: Gun Violence Archive

Places Where Mass Shootings Occur

The specific settings in which mass shootings occur provide clues as to the motives. Shootings in the home usually involve a domestic issue or a dispute at a private gathering. An incident at a nightclub often points to a spontaneous or ongoing dispute. A mass shooting at a school may involve a former or current student with personal grievances against fellow students or school staff.

Table 23 illustrates that in 2019–2020 the most frequent location of a mass shooting was the street or highway, accounting for nearly a third of all incidents. The next most common location was in or around a home, including an apartment. This was followed in frequency by a bar or club or some other business (e.g., gas station, restaurant, convenience store, or facility used for a gathering). Other common locations for mass shootings were cars, parks and playgrounds, parking lots, and the grounds of apartment complexes. The table lists all the locations that appeared more than twice.

It is noteworthy that out of the total of 1,029 mass shootings, 713 (69.2%) took place on the street, in or around a residence, or in or around a bar or club. With the exception of bars and restaurants serving alcohol, which are subject to prohibitions in about half the states with regard to the carrying of guns, the most common locations of mass shootings are those in which civilian gun carrying is usually allowed. Streets, residences, most businesses, private vehicles, parks, apartment complex grounds, and parking lots are all places that tend not to be subject to federal or state prohibitions.

Therefore, the present study is consistent with previous research showing that the overwhelming majority of mass shootings do not occur in so-called "gun-free" zones. This false narrative has been promoted by groups and individuals advocating the further expansion of gun carrying. Their argument is that zones prohibiting civilian gun carrying invite mass shootings as people in these settings cannot defend themselves. Thus, they argue that most restrictions on carrying should be dropped. Clearly, the data show that prohibitions on carrying are not a determining factor as to the location of these incidents as most occur in places in which gun carrying is permitted.

As many shootings occur in public spaces or in or around businesses, steps can be taken to make these environments less hospitable to gun violence and mass shootings. For example, environments can be designed and modified to prevent crime (see Chapter 6). One noteworthy finding was that relative to other settings, schools and college/university campuses were rarely the site of mass shootings. This finding suggests that, while remaining ever-vigilant, schools might reconsider drills that can be traumatic for students and states ought to reflect on the perils of arming school staff.

Table 23. Location of Mass Shootings, 2019-2020

LOCATION	NUMBER OF CASES*	% OF CASES
STREET/ROAD	324	31.5
IN/AROUND RESIDENCE	278	27.0
IN/AROUND BAR OR CLUB	111 (10 clubs were unlicensed)	10.8
OTHER BUSINESS	100	9.7
CAR	51	5.0
PARK/PLAYGROUND/FIELD	48	4.7
APARTMENT COMPLEX	47	4.6
PARKING LOT	46	4.5
UNIVERSITY/SCHOOL	6	.6
ENTERTAINMENT DISTRICT/STADIUM/EVENT CENTER	6	.6
COMMUNITY/RECREATIONAL CENTER	4	.4
BUS STOP/BUS	4	.4
MALL	4	.4
OTHER LOCATIONS	15	1.5

Source: Gun Violence Archive

*The number of locations exceeds the number of cases in the study as some mass shootings spilled over into a second location. For example, a shooting in a home or of victims in a car occasionally continued outside on the street.

Circumstances and Motives of Mass Shootings

Table 24 details the circumstances and motives of mass shootings in 2019–2020. The range of motives and features illustrates the wide variety of these incidents. Gatherings, such as parties and cookouts, served as the most frequent contexts for the mass shootings, accounting for almost a quarter of all cases. Such gatherings occurred in homes, in public spaces, and at businesses and venues specializing in these events. Dozens of shootings occurred in very large gatherings, especially following the lockdowns prompted by the Covid-19 pandemic.

The most frequent motive, mentioned in over one in five cases, was an ongoing or spontaneous dispute or altercation at a residence, in a public place, or at a business. This motive was likely far more prevalent as the lack of an explicit reference to a dispute in source materials is no guarantee that no dispute took place prior to a shooting. In reality, we might imagine that most mass shootings, whether at a party, a drive-by shooting, a domestic shooting, or a gang-related mass shooting, is the culmination of some form of conflict. Drive-by shootings were the next most frequent feature, though they represent a form of attack rather than a motive. Many of these shootings are unsolved as the suspects tend to pull up to a location, fire their weapons, and drive off. One can only assume that they represent some form of planned hit as no provocation normally occurs at the time of the shooting.

Close to 10% of the shootings were explicitly referred to as group- or gang-related. Many groups are neighborhood based rather than large formal gangs like the Bloods or Crips. This category may be far more common but there is no way of knowing whether some of the unsolved drive-by shootings or some of the other unsolved cases were group-related. The next most frequent category, targeted shootings, also are likely to be undercounted as shootings were only said to be targeted if source materials on the incident made explicit reference to the targeting of specific victims. Close to 5% of the cases involved shootouts or exchanges of gunfire, and a similar number involved a domestic/intimate relationship.

A smaller number of cases involved some form of criminal activity, such as the drug trade, a robbery, home invasion, a hate crime, or terrorism. According to the source materials available, mass shootings involving mentally ill suspects, random shootings, and workplace shootings each accounted for no more than 1% of the cases. Therefore, mass shootings involving these factors or motives were fewer than is commonly believed.

After examining more than a thousand mass shootings that occurred in 2019–2020, what was especially striking were the many cases in which the perpetrators recklessly shot into groups of people and appeared to be indifferent to uninvolved bystanders who might also get hit. The emotional volatility of shooters was also noteworthy. For example, in Copiague, New York on December 12, 2020, a 62-year-old customer at a deli heard someone make a comment about him, pulled out a 9mm handgun, and shot four people, killing two of them.[169] The deli owner, an innocent bystander, was one of those killed in the shooting. In downtown Nashville on November 8, 2020, two men began to argue about a dog owned by one of them. The man with the dog pulled out a gun during the dispute. The second suspect then left the scene but returned with a gun and accompanied by several men. An exchange of gunfire ensued, with eight individuals and the dog being shot.[170]

Following a mass shooting in October 2020, Atlanta interim Police Chief Rodney Bryant observed that people were having more difficulty resolving conflicts during the pandemic.[171] In 2020, firing into a large crowd was not uncommon, even in shootings in which specific individuals were targeted. Law enforcement officials and members of the public often commented on the seeming recklessness and senselessness of many shootings and the general indifference to life. Following a drive-by shooting outside a Milwaukee funeral home in September 2020, the acting police chief said: "This brazen act that was done in broad daylight is just unacceptable in our city.... The city's mayor added: "The insanity of people solving their problems with guns...we are seeing way too much of that in the community this year."[172]

Our sources also indicated that, following mass shootings, potential witnesses often left the scene and withheld their cooperation from the police. As will be discussed in Chapter 6, such lack of cooperation is a symptom, in part, of an absence of perceived police legitimacy in these neighborhoods. Where police are viewed with suspicion, hostility, and fear, cases are less likely to be solved as public cooperation is critical to the solution of most criminal cases. A low solution rate, in turn, emboldens those contemplating the use of lethal violence.

Table 24. Circumstances/Features of Mass Shootings, 2019–2020

MOTIVE/NATURE	NUMBER OF CASES*	% OF CASES*
PARTY/GATHERING	253	24.6
DISPUTE/ALTERCATION	229	22.3
DRIVE-BY SHOOTING	192	18.7
GANG/GROUP CONFLICT	97	9.4
TARGETED SHOOTING	58	5.6
SHOOTOUT	50	4.9
DOMESTIC/INTIMATE RELATIONSHIP	48	4.7
DRUG-INVOLVED SHOOTING/RAID	32	3.1
MURDER-SUICIDE OR SUICIDE OF SHOOTER	19	1.8
HOME INVASION	19	1.8
RETALIATION	17	1.7
SPREE SHOOTING	15	1.5
MENTALLY ILL/UNSTABLE SHOOTER	11	1.1
DEFENSIVE SHOOTING OR GUN USE	10	1.0
ROBBERY	5	.5
ROAD RAGE	5	.5
WORKPLACE GRIEVANCE	4	.4
HATE CRIME	4	.4
RANDOM SHOOTING	4	.4
TERRORISM	1	.1
OTHERS	4	.4

Source: Gun Violence Archive

*This column exceeds 100% as many cases involve more than one feature—e.g., dispute at a party. Also, the fact that a feature (e.g., a dispute) was not mentioned in source materials does not nmean that such a feature was not present.

Table 25 summarizes the most common settings and features/motives of mass shootings occurring in 2019–2020. The locations in which mass shootings occur are a mix of public and private. The most common settings were public streets and parks; private homes and cars; and privately owned businesses such as bars and gas stations. The most common features of mass shootings were parties and other gatherings—many of them large ones—disputes, drive-by shootings (more a way of carrying out a shooting than a motive), gang/group conflict, targeted shootings that may or may not be group-related, and shootings within the context of an intimate partner relationship or one that has recently ended.

When the cases were examined to determine which combinations of settings and features were most frequently observed, the following patterns emerged:

- Shootings at parties/gatherings held on the street, with or without a reference to a dispute;
- Drive-by shootings on the street, with or without a reference to a party/gathering;
- Drive-by shootings at a residence;
- Shootings following a dispute on the street;
- Shootings at parties or other meetings held in the home, with or without a reference to a dispute;
- Shootings at parties/gatherings held in a park;
- Shootings of family members in a residence;
- Shootings in/around a bar/club following a dispute, with or without a reference to a party or gang. These cases sometimes involved a perpetrator who was denied entry or asked to leave.

Table 25. Predominant Sites and Features of Mass Shootings, 2019–2020

LOCATION	MOTIVE/FEATURE
STREET/ROAD	Party/gathering
IN/AROUND RESIDENCE	Dispute/altercation
IN/AROUND BAR OR CLUB	Drive-by shooting
OTHER BUSINESS	Gang/group conflict
CAR	Targeted shooting
PARK/PLAYGROUND/FIELD	Domestic/intimate relationship
PARKING LOT	
APARTMENT COMPLEX	

6
Preventing Mass Shootings:
Social, Economic and Cultural Reforms

The media's selective coverage of mass shootings and focus on the deadliest events, as well as those affecting the majority White population, has presented a distorted view of these tragedies. When considering mass shootings, most people think of Columbine, Las Vegas, El Paso, Sandy Hook, Parkland, Orlando, and San Bernardino. These were planned events in which the shooters, either enraged at a specific group or society in general—"hunting humans" as one shooter referred to it— aimed to inflict a maximum of casualties.

While the high-profile, high-casualty shootings just mentioned receive the bulk of the media's attention, the vast majority of mass shootings, when defined as they are in this book, are very different. Many involve little or no planning and do not involve indiscriminately shooting to maximize the body count. Shootings often involve recklessness and bystanders can be hurt, but this is not by design. Most arise from disputes, whether ongoing or spontaneous, and the goal is to settle scores with specific people. When guns are deployed at a party, other gathering, or a bar, when high-powered weapons are used, and/or when gunfire is exchanged in a crowded space, bystanders are likely to get hurt. While mass shootings occur in communities of every size and in virtually every state, they occur disproportionately in communities of color, especially in certain African American neighborhoods.

Among the surprises in the study conducted for this book is that, even in America, large-scale school attacks, terrorism, hate crimes, and other massacres in which people are shot randomly are relatively few in number. Louis Klarevas of Columbia University tracked gun massacres (six or more killed excluding the perpetrator) occurring between 1966 and 2015 and found 111 over the 50-year period, just over two incidents per year.[173] Our own study, covering 2019 and 2020, identified 31 high-casualty incidents (six or more killed and/or 10 shot) for these record-breaking years, just over one per month.

There were three random mass shootings in all in a school or university campus in 2019–2020 and none of these incidents approached the scale of the Columbine, Sandy Hook, or Marjory Stoneman Douglas slaughters. The rarity of large-scale school attacks is supported by a US Secret Service study that identified a total of 10 mass attacks on schools (three or more injured or killed, excluding the attacker) over a 10-year period (2008–2017).[174] Schools might still be advised to control access, conduct threat assessments, foster a climate of inclusion, and make psychological interventions available to at-risk students. However, excessively "realistic" active shooter drills that traumatize children, make them fear school, and impact classroom performance should be reconsidered given the extremely low probability of a major attack on any given school.

Mass shootings motivated by hate against an identifiable group were also few in number as they accounted for just three out of the 1,029 incidents in 2019–2020. These shootings, though, tended to be especially devastating in the casualties they produced. The El Paso (Texas) Walmart attack, committed by a White supremacist with a grudge against Hispanic Americans, killed 23 people and injured another 23. Former President Donald Trump's hateful rhetoric against Mexicans and immigrants has energized White supremacist groups and likely influenced the 21-year-old shooter. Trump repeatedly referred to immigrants heading for the southern border as an invasion. The El Paso shooter railed against immigration and stated that his attack was a response "to the Hispanic invasion of Texas,"[175] Hate crimes like this mass shooting increased during Trump's tenure, and avoiding incendiary rhetoric originating from the highest offices in the US is one obvious step in reversing this trend.

Domestic incidents accounted for 48 (4.7%) of the mass shootings in 2019–2020. Previous studies have suggested that domestic incidents make up a far higher percentage of mass shootings. The group Everytown for Gun Safety studied mass shootings (which they defined as four or more killed, excluding the shooter) and found that seven in 10 occurred exclusively or in part in the home.[176] More than half involved a current or former intimate partner or family member. The differences in definition may account for some of the discrepancy between the two studies as domestic shootings are more likely to reach the threshold of four or more people killed than other types of shootings and, hence, to be classified by Everytown as a mass shooting. Domestic mass shootings are also more likely to result in the wounding and death of children than other shootings.

Workplace shootings too have much notoriety and, in the 1980s, following a spate of shootings involving postal workers, the term "going postal" came to refer to aggrieved workers who showed up at their current or former workplace and murdered superiors and/or colleagues. Again, there were very few of these incidents relative to other categories of mass shootings. In 2019–2020, there were four workplace shootings, less than one percent of all mass shootings over the two-year study period.

Two high-casualty workplace shootings, one in Aurora (Illinois) and the other in Virginia Beach (Virginia), while different, had some common features. In Aurora, G. Martin attended a disciplinary hearing and anticipated that he might be fired at that hearing.[177] When he was fired, he shot fellow employees at the hearing. He was able to bring a firearm into the warehouse in which he worked and then to bring it with him to the meeting. On the morning of the shooting, Martin had informed another co-worker that he would kill every other employee and "blow police up." He issued such threats regularly. Martin wounded five responding police officers.

D. Craddock, perpetrator of the shooting at the Virginia Beach Municipal Center, also was going through a transition as he submitted a letter of resignation the morning of his attack. He displayed no discipline problems, but an investigation revealed that Craddock was isolated and paranoid, felt he was being treated unfairly by the city, and had problems with work performance.[178] He, too, was able to bring firearms into the workplace. Unlike Martin, Craddock did not appear to verbalize his sense of grievance toward the employer.

While every case of workplace violence is unique, these two cases illustrate the role of dismissal or a resignation as a precursor to a shooting. Both sensitivity and vigilance ought to be exercised at these times, as a transition from a career position often will have a significant social, psychological, and economic impact on an individual. Workplace policies that prohibit the carrying of firearms into the setting and practices to enforce such policies can help avert these tragedies. Practices that allow workers to air grievances and identify blind spots in terms of the treatment of personnel can potentially allow issues to be identified before they reach a boiling point. Where threats are made, as in Aurora, employees ought to be trained not to ignore them and employers should conduct threat assessments to determine the likelihood that threats will be translated into action.

While police and media sources do not provide a complete picture of suspects, just 11 (1.1%) of the mass shootings in 2019–2020 suggest that mental illness or serious instability were factors in the shootings. This supports the general literature that, as indicated in Chapter Four, shows that less than 3% of violence is due to serious mental illness. In just one of the high-casualty incidents in the two-year period, the Dayton, Ohio mass shooting in August 2019, did sources specifically note that the shooter complained of auditory and visual hallucinations.[179]

While mental illness is not a factor in most mass shootings, educational, work, and other environments need to encourage people to come forward if they learn of someone who discusses disturbing thoughts of violence or issues threats, especially if that person has a history of violence and has acquired weapons. When notified, organizations should have the capacity to undertake expeditious threat assessments. Extreme risk laws can also be useful in providing a legal avenue, for those close to such a person, to petition a court to remove firearms from the possession of those deemed to be a threat to themselves or others. C. Betts, the Dayton shooter, not only exhibited psychotic episodes but was a substance abuser and fascinated by violence.[180] In fact, classmates report that he maintained a list of individuals he hoped to kill or rape. Psychiatric intervention, drug counseling, and removing his access to firearms might have averted the tragedy in Dayton.

The present study has shown that most mass shootings do not involve school attacks, hate crimes, mental illness, workplace grievances, terrorism (just one case), or domestic violence. The vast majority in which a motive could be ascertained involved a dispute, whether ongoing or spontaneous, that escalated due to the presence of lethal weapons. The non-domestic disputes most often took place on the street, in the home, or at a bar/club. Disputes may involve individuals or groups of people. Many mass shootings occurred at parties or gatherings and, in the Covid-19 period, dozens of shootings occurred at very large gatherings. There were also many drive-by shootings in which the victims have been shot on the street, in front of homes, or in stationary or moving vehicles. The motives in such shootings are often difficult to ascertain as often these incidents are not solved. Some drive-bys are group- or gang-related, while many involve people firing into crowds with little information as to the motives or whether specific individuals are being targeted.

The media, social scientists, and activists have virtually ignored the daily shootings in urban areas, which terrorize communities, especially those of color. These daily shootings often occur in public spaces, such as streets, parks, and outside homes and nightclubs. This poses challenges for prevention because, unlike facilities like schools, controlling access and securing public spaces raises a multitude of logistical and even human rights concerns. While schools can be equipped with cameras, control access during the day, and establish security procedures, comparable actions in public spaces are either not possible or may be viewed as encroaching on the freedom of the public to move around without being under surveillance. Still, if the political will is present, many measures can be taken to reduce the incidence of mass shootings even in public spaces.

Does the political will exist in the US to stop the carnage? The jury is still out. However, Australia, a country with a frontier history, strong gun lobby and culture, and a federalist system of government, showed that there is another way forward. Until 1996, gun laws varied by state. Following a catastrophic shooting spree in which 35 people were killed and 23 wounded by a sole gunman, then Prime Minister John Howard, a conservative, concluded that major gun law reforms were needed. Facing considerable resistance from his own supporters and even assassination threats, Howard pressured the states to forge an agreement that radically transformed Australia's gun laws. Among the reforms was the creation of a national firearm licensing and registration system, as well as a ban on automatic and semiautomatic long guns, the latter often being used in mass shootings. The government bought back and melted down a fifth to a third of all firearms in the country. The law reforms appeared to have a dramatic effect as there have been just three mass shootings in the last 23 years, only one of which occurred in a public place.[181]

Howard doubts that Americans have the will to follow Australia's bold measures on firearms. He writes: "Millions of law-abiding Americans truly believe that it is safer to own a gun, based on the chilling logic that because there are so many guns in circulation, one's own weapon is needed for self-protection. To put it another way, the situation is so far gone there can be no turning back."[182]

Public will is critical as the police, in the performance of their routine duties, cannot be expected to achieve success on their own. Preventive measures must be implemented and legal reforms enacted to achieve significant change.

Law Enforcement Initiatives and Limits

When a mass shooting occurs, local police and emergency medical personnel tend to be the first official responders on the scene. Law enforcement will engage the suspect(s), establish control over the crime scene, rescue victims, create a perimeter to preserve evidence and keep bystanders at a distance, facilitate removal of the injured, and set up procedures for notifying and dealing with concerned family members. They will also provide updates to the public via traditional and social media.

Law enforcement's responsibilities in these areas and their availability around-the-clock makes them the primary contact for media interviews. The downside is that media coverage is limited for all but the most horrific mass shootings, and most reporters will file their stories once they have interviewed local police and possibly a security consultant. The result is that the public is exposed primarily to stories focusing on the number of victims, the suspect and how he committed the offense, how he was captured or killed, and how various security measures may have prevented the horror. Usually, little attention is paid to criminologists and other social scientists with knowledge about the roots of violence and a better understanding of broader social measures that may prevent such shootings. The primary responsibility of the police is not to understand these incidents but to stabilize the crime scene, apprehend or incapacitate the suspect, and collect and preserve evidence.

While modern police departments strive to solve community problems and to be proactive in preventing crime, policing is still largely a reactive undertaking in which departments respond following a call by a member of the community. In the US, the chief law enforcement officer of a county is the sheriff and this is usually an elected position. As a result, county law enforcement is incentivized to be responsive to the population at large as the failure to serve the public in a timely manner jeopardizes the sheriff's re-election. Responding promptly to public complaints is more visible than preventive patrol and other proactive measures. Hence, reacting to crime will normally take precedence over crime prevention and solving community problems (e.g., disputes that can escalate between spouses, neighbors, or neighborhood groups).

Police primarily are involved in the suppression of crime rather than in the understanding and preventing of it. If they were highly effective in preventing crime one would expect that neighborhoods persistently receiving the highest levels of surveillance and enforcement activity would have the lowest rates of crime and violence. Usually the opposite is the case. Research on the effectiveness of traditional policing activities fails to provide evidence that adding police, preventive patrol, or faster response times following calls have an impact on crime. [183] Most violent crimes and mass shootings are over by the time police respond despite the fact that response times to mass shootings tend to be very short. However, many mass shootings are over in under a minute.

In the 2019 Dayton, Ohio shooting, patrolling police officers shot the perpetrator 30 seconds after the first shot was fired but, by then, nine individuals were killed and 27 others were wounded. [184] In 2018, the MSD High School shooter in Parkland, Florida fired 136 rounds in six minutes. In less than two minutes, he had already shot or killed 23 people on the first floor of the building he entered. [185] The 2012 Aurora, Colorado movie theater shooting was over in two minutes but, by then, 70 people were killed or wounded. [186] The US Secret Service has found that most school attacks are over in two minutes or less. [187]

Law enforcement and private security firms can make use of gunshot detection technology, which alerts them to a shooting as soon as a shot is fired in public, a mall, or other facility. This technology uses acoustic-based sensors (microphones) or ultrasonic sensors, which detect the concussive wave created by a bullet. [188] The aim is to allow responding police or security personnel to be notified faster than is the case when first responders wait to be notified by victims or bystanders. When coupled with video management systems, such technologies can identify the suspect and his location, thereby enabling an efficient response by police or security personnel.

These technologies have a number of downsides. False alerts stemming from such things as ambient sounds (background noises) lead to the unnecessary deployment of resources, raising the cost of such a system. Research fails to find that gunshot detection technology actually speeds up police response times or reduces crime rates in neighborhoods in which it is implemented.[189,190] The technology is not applicable to the many shootings that occur in homes or small businesses (bars). Experiments with the acoustic-based technology have tended to be conducted in high-crime areas already subject to more intensive police surveillance than other areas. The residents of such communities are often people of color who may resent a further extension of police power in neighborhoods already receiving more scrutiny than other communities. Community cooperation is required for effective policing. Gunshot detection technology is also a completely reactive tool that does not address the roots of the violence.

Dawud Walid, Michigan executive director of the Council on American Islamic Relations, notes that there is apprehension about the overreach of such technologies and states that gun violence "can't be policed away." Mr. Walid adds: "Spending more money on law enforcement and technology is not dealing with the real issues that people need to make communities safer.... Social services, afterschool programs, and community centers bring more stability to neighborhoods, not more police carrying guns."[191]

Importance of Police Legitimacy

While law enforcement represents a small part of the solution to mass shootings, police behavior does have a significant role to play in the respect of citizens for the law and in solving crimes. Criminologists have known for decades that most crime is not solved by the police acting alone but, rather, with the indispensable information provided by the public. In many cases reviewed by this writer, the police appealed to the public for information as witnesses had left the scene or failed to cooperate. When the police are viewed as a hostile force rather than as a legitimate source of authority, community members are less likely to come forward with information, fewer crimes will be solved, and aggressors therefore know that they can commit acts of violence with virtual impunity. Without the cooperation of witnesses, it is difficult for law enforcement to ascertain the motives and identify suspects.

The "Ferguson Effect," the observation that violence increased following the police killings of Michael Brown in Ferguson, Missouri and George Floyd in Minneapolis, among other cases, illustrates that perceived gross misuses of force activate longstanding cynicism toward the police among communities of color. Communities may experience more violence and tend to withdraw their cooperation from the police. The result is more crime followed by greater repression by police, creating a vicious cycle.

In October 2004, Frank Jude, a Black man, attended a party hosted by some Milwaukee police officers, all of whom were White. Feeling uncomfortable, Jude decided to leave but was accused of stealing. He was brutally attacked by the officers and the incident became a front-page story in the *Milwaukee Journal Sentinel.* In the year following the publication of the story, calls to police declined by 17% and most of this decline came from African American neighborhoods.[192] In addition, the homicide rate in Milwaukee increased by 32% following the story's appearance in the newspaper. Community cynicism, in turn, further increases when the police are seen as unable to protect residents of the affected community. Using survey data, researchers David Kirk and Andrew Papachristos have found that neighborhoods reporting high levels of legal cynicism have significantly higher homicide rates than those viewing police and the law more favorably.[193] Legal cynicism was more closely correlated with violence than poverty or unemployment. Unfavorable attitudes toward the police also makes it more likely that an individual will carry a gun.

Interviews with youth and young adults at high risk of violence in New York City and testimony from Chicago gang experts reveal the extent to which some communities, especially those of color, distrust the police. In general, the youth felt police did not care about the community and that they were often being stopped for low-level crime while nothing was being done about serious crime. They often felt that police treated them as less than human and that race was a major factor in the maltreatment. In addition, the youth and young men indicated that they carried guns both to protect themselves from aggressors in the community and as protection from the police. Said a 24-year-old Black man: "You gotta protect your life because the cops might shoot you."[194] A study of gangs in Chicago found that youth often see the city's police department as more a part of the problem than a solution. As a result, youth involved in a dispute believe that they have to take "justice" into their own hands.[195]

Many of the mass shootings seen in 2019–2020 arose from ongoing disputes between individuals and groups. In communities with a high regard for the police, residents will be more likely to seek the assistance of officers in mediating and resolving conflicts. Where the police are viewed with suspicion and hostility, or are viewed as corrupt or as indifferent, "street justice" will prevail more frequently, meaning that individuals or groups will retaliate against those with whom they have a conflict. Many mass shootings fall in this category.

How do police departments enhance their legitimacy in the eyes of the community they police? Procedural justice is important, meaning that residents must feel that their interactions with the police are fair and that officers apply the law in a neutral manner, treating citizens with dignity and respect.[196] Interactions consistent with procedural justice include such things as allowing people to provide their perspective of an incident, explaining what will happen to suspects and why, and making sure they understand their rights. Police training must incorporate the principles and techniques of procedural justice. Training must include techniques in the de-escalation of conflicts and raise officer awareness of the impact of the use of excessive force on relations with the community. Providing assistance to community members by informing them of services available to them or by offering comfort, where appropriate, also raises the community's level of trust in relation to a department or officer.

Dialogue with the community is another critical aspect of police legitimacy. Measures to improve community dialogue include:

- increasing the presence of police in the community through such measures as foot patrols so officers and community residents become more familiar with one another;
- creating citizen advisory boards that provide feedback as to community sentiment on policing matters;
- having citizen representation on commissions investigating police misconduct;
- participating in restorative justice conferences involving the police, an offender, and victim at which the aim is to identify suitable restitution to a victim following a lower-level offense; and,
- having police attend important community events, such as town hall meetings, as well as sporting events involving young people. [197]

Focused Deterrence

One initiative shown to have a consistent impact on crime and violence is focused deterrence. A study of 43 reviews covering 1,400 individual studies has found that focused deterrence had the strongest and most consistent anti-violence effects, including gang violence, street crime driven by drug markets, and individual offending.[198] This strategy was first implemented in Boston's Operation Ceasefire project. Researchers had diagnosed the youth gun violence problem in Boston as one of largely vendetta-like conflicts among a small population of chronic offenders who were responsible for the majority of youth homicides in the city. With this strategy, the police and community representatives engage with those at high risk of committing acts of violence and communicate the consequences should they continue their violent behavior. These consequences (deterrents) include enhanced prosecution and penalties for violent and low-level offenses going forward. At the same time, they are informed of incentives to refrain from violence as they are offered services like job training and drug treatment. This carrot-and-stick approach aims to deflect people away from crime and improve police-community relations through a tough but compassionate and procedurally fair approach.[199]

Typically, a focused deterrence strategy will need the following staffing:[200]

- an interagency enforcement group comprising police, probation and parole agencies, and prosecutors to coordinate the strategy;
- a research and evaluation group to track how well the strategy is working and identify and resolve problems;
- an analysis and intelligence team to identify the high-risk offenders to be included in the intervention;
- a team to run communications efforts with the individuals and groups who will receive the intervention;
- an enforcement team, including law enforcement and prosecutors, to carry out enforcement efforts for individuals and groups persisting in criminal behavior;
- a team of community outreach workers and case managers to coordinate services for those choosing to move away from crime and violence.

Evaluations of focused deterrence have tended to yield large reductions in violent crime. Boston experienced a 63% reduction in youth homicides, Stockton (California) experienced a 42% reduction in gun homicides, and New Haven (Connecticut) saw shootings decline by 73%.[201] The strategy appears to work because it combines threats of sanctions communicated directly to offenders (deterrence) and concrete assistance offers to individuals and groups, thereby conferring legitimacy on the initiative.

Violence Interruption

The present study on mass shootings in 2019–2020 illustrates that much violence involves conflicts and cycles of retaliation among individuals and small groups. One immediate way of preventing violence is interrupting these cycles by working with people who have been victimized or those who may seek revenge on behalf of the injured or deceased individual.

Hospital-based violence intervention programs seek to reduce violence by focusing on high-risk individuals recently admitted to a hospital for a violent injury. Medical professionals know that being the victim of a violent injury makes it far more likely that the person will return with a subsequent injury or become a perpetrator of violence.[202] Hospitalization for a serious injury may represent a unique opportunity to intervene positively. Currently, hospitals discharge patients injured from gunshot wounds without any strategy to address the increased likelihood of violence.

Patients are screened to identify those at greatest risk and matched with case managers who provide intense oversight in the hospital and the critical months following their release from hospital. At the same time, the case managers help connect their clients with community agencies providing a range of services, introducing high-risk individuals to a variety of community-based organizations to give them access to employment, housing, and educational resources. An evaluation of the YouthAlive! Program in Oakland, California found its clients were 70% less likely to be arrested and 60% less likely to have any criminal involvement compared to a control group.[203] A Baltimore program found that just 5% of participating patients were re-injured, compared to 36% for non-participants. Participants were also four times less likely to be convicted of a crime than non-participants.[204]

A program developed in Chicago, Cure Violence, also has a critical component involving violence interruption. This program is rooted in the idea that violence is akin to a contagious disease that is transmitted in the community through imitation and social norms. It is believed that this transmission can be interrupted to slow the spread of the violence. America's poor, inner-city neighborhoods are seen as the epicenters of the gun violence epidemic.

The program recruits "Violence Interrupters" to detect and resolve potentially violent conflicts.[205] The aim is to prevent retaliation in response to previous violence and to mediate conflicts. To build trust, these individuals are from the same neighborhood as those being targeted by the program. Effective interrupters often engaged in high-risk behavior themselves, including gang membership. They spend much of their time working in the streets, making connections, and building trust with those most at risk for violence. Through community networks, they learn about conflicts that may turn violent.

The Cure Violence program also places an emphasis on changing community-level social norms that promote violence by educating and mobilizing community members, including clergy members, business owners, school leaders, politicians, and residents. The aim is to encourage community members to promote positive change and peaceful conflict resolution. Public education in the form of campaigns supporting peaceful conflict resolution is also critical (e.g., flyers, billboards, and bumper stickers with concise, easy-to-understand messages).

While evaluations of the Cure Violence program are mixed, some jurisdictions have found shootings to decline by over 60%. The approach has been rated as promising and is viewed as cost-efficient, placing a low level of demand on law enforcement and criminal justice system resources.[206]

Improving the Physical Environment

Urban planner Jane Jacobs was a pioneer in showing that the physical environment played a role in the level of crime and violence in a neighborhood. In her seminal work, *The Death and Life of Great American Cities*, published in 1961, Jacobs showed that communities with an abundance of pedestrian traffic and diversity in land use were safer than those with less vitality.[207] From the 1970s, criminologists, as well as several architects, have made the case that reshaping the physical environment, from entire communities to housing projects and shopping malls, could make it less hospitable to crime.

Design principles that will make an area less conducive to crime and violence include:

- Surveillance—building design, lighting, and landscape can make it more likely that people who commit acts of violence can be seen;
- Access Control—walkways, fences, and landscape can keep unauthorized people and weapons out of certain places, such as schools, government buildings, and other sensitive areas;
- Territorial Reinforcement—design features such as pavement, landscaping, and signage that communicate that an area is out of bounds and under the control of a municipality, business, or residents;
- Maintenance—properties that have been neglected seem to be magnets for criminal behavior as they convey the sense that no one cares about the area or building and, hence, no consequences will ensue if illicit behavior occurs.[208]

Our analysis of mass shootings in 2019–2020 revealed that a significant number occurred in nuisance establishments (e.g., bars with multiple occurrences of violence) and in places that did not incorporate the design principles just mentioned. Many shootings occurred on the street in the evenings or overnight (when visibility is lower), in parking lots, in abandoned lots, or in abandoned buildings. While some perpetrators will not be deterred by any design feature, the vast majority of mass shooting suspects fled from the scene and sought to escape arrest. Therefore, most of the shooters were not indifferent to the risks associated with their conduct.

While modification of the physical environment alone does not address the motivation of perpetrators—the "why" of violence—it can reduce opportunities for violence and help make communities more healthy and cohesive places. Opportunities for illegal gun and drug dealing can be reduced and the fear associated with common nuisances can also be lowered.

Promising research in this area includes:

- Increasing greening in Chicago public housing areas was associated with significantly less violent crime;
- Converting vacant lots into parks has yielded positive outcomes as it indicates to residents that communities are closely monitoring new green spaces. Among other things, greening vacant lots may prevent gun assaults as such areas are known to be used for the storage and disposal of illegal guns;
- A major "cleaning and greening" initiative in Philadelphia involving vacant lots revealed that removing trash and debris, grading the land, planting grass and a small number of trees to create a park-like setting, installing perimeter fences, and maintaining lots on a regular basis reduced community safety concerns considerably and was associated with a reduction in gun violence of 17%. Community pride also can be enhanced;

- Another Philadelphia study found that the remediation of abandoned buildings was associated with a 39% reduction in gun assaults;
- A review of improved street lighting across eight American and five British studies concluded that crime overall, including violent crime, decreased by 20% when compared to areas not benefitting from such improvements.[209]

Aside from nuisance locations, like certain vacant lots, there are operating businesses, such as bars and lounges, that are notorious for repeated violence. Our study showed that a significant number of mass shootings occurred in or around these establishments in 2019–2020. In some cases, witnesses or the police indicated that the present mass shooting was just the most recent in a history of violence and shootings at that location. Municipal officials can act to revoke the license of nuisance establishments. Kansas City, Missouri, shut down a lounge after two mass shootings there in 2020.[210] Communities would be wise to take an aggressive stand against places that seem to be a point of convergence for individuals and groups that have displayed a propensity toward violence and that may have an ongoing beef with others also patronizing that establishment.

Tackling Persistent and Concentrated Poverty

Table 7 in Chapter 4 showed dramatically the extent to which some American cities are distressed, meaning that a significant percentage of their neighborhoods have a high concentration of poverty, joblessness, few economic prospects locally, and many residents without even a high school diploma. The table also shows that cities in which over a third of the neighborhoods are rated as distressed (e.g., Detroit, Chicago, Baltimore) have much higher homicide rates than those in which fewer neighborhoods are distressed (New York, Los Angeles). The persistence of poverty and other social problems for African Americans is illustrated by the fact that the homicide rate in places like Chicago for Blacks is about the same as it was in the 1930s.[211]

While this is not a short-term endeavor, there is no getting around the impact of poverty and despair on the many mass shootings in 2019–2020 in which spontaneous disputes rapidly escalated to gunfire. Or the many drive-by and other shootings in which the shooter showed an utter disregard for human life and wounded or killed bystanders, including infants. This volatility of disputes and indifference to others reflects a sense of hopelessness in which little value is placed on human life, including one's own. Dozens of mass shootings of this type in Chicago, Baltimore, St. Louis, and other cities indicate that hopelessness has metastasized in certain communities and its roots must be confronted. There are no easy fixes. As discussed in Chapter 4, a combination of decline in America's industrial sector, global forces, disinvestment in certain communities, especially communities of color, and racial segregation have left some communities with high levels of joblessness and few opportunities for young people.

Rachel Swaner and her colleagues in New York City interviewed youth and young men at risk in some of the city's most violent neighborhoods. Interviewed youth noted that economic stresses on them and their families led them to commit robberies and engage in drug dealing and confirmed that these activities required guns. They didn't romanticize these activities. Said one Latino youth: "Cause when you broke, you get angry about everything and then you grab your gun and just do robberies and do stuff you not supposed to be doing to get your money."[212] Another youth added: "We gotta make our money happen. And one thing I can say, they don't make it nice for a Black man to live out here. You gotta make your own heaven out here."[213] Swaner and her team recommend bringing services, like job programs, to the youth as gang and other rivalries may keep them from traveling outside their neighborhoods.

A report by the Great Cities Institute of the University of Illinois in Chicago notes that persistent disinvestment and concentrated poverty represents an assault on the dignity and self-worth of Black youth and is associated with violence.[214] The authors note that prevention programs need to counter codes of hypermasculinity with the means to restore dignity and self-worth, teach healing and conflict resolution, while advocating for economic and educational opportunities. Hypermasculinity codes involve hypersensitivity to insult, which in turn is a result of "ongoing, institutionalized assault" on a person's self-worth and dignity. The assault on dignity stems from household and neighborhood socioeconomic conditions in areas where homicide rates are highest. Rooted in persistent and concentrated poverty, hypermasculinity codes help explain the anger and readiness to fight and shoot at the slightest provocation. People are on edge—even more so during the pandemic—and defending their honor. Our study of 2019–2020 has revealed many mass shootings sparked by arguments that have arisen spontaneously.

Focusing on Conflict Resolution Rather than Gangs

A compelling analysis of violence in Chicago by scholars with a deep familiarity with the city makes the point that the city today, like other rust belt urban centers, has seen gangs or cliques organized along neighborhood lines.[215] These are smaller groupings in which members have greater autonomy rather than top-down entities. In any event, much violence is not seen as gang-related at all but a result of personal disputes and retaliation. This is consistent with our finding that many mass shootings involve personal disputes. While neighborhoods in Chicago vary, much violence is not related to drug markets or gang rivalries. The authors argue that the focus in anti-violence efforts should be on conflict resolution and community economic development rather than gangs. Anti-violence efforts need to distinguish between identity and drug-related violence.

The group of Chicago-based scholars note that many African American gangs today are horizontally organized neighborhood cliques with little or no formal leadership structure. Rather than being ordered by gang leaders, violence is more spontaneous and tends to be initiated by individuals. For example, youth interviewed in three of New York's most violent neighborhoods talk about their constant conflicts over drugs, money, girls, and disrespect.[216] The capacity of the new cliques to mediate internal and neighborhood conflicts has diminished. Measures focusing on gang leaders and non-existent gang structures are out of date and ineffective. Efforts need to address hypermasculinity codes and mediating interpersonal conflicts, in the context of considerable economic development.

The fracturing of traditional gangs in Chicago occurred due to the end of the crack epidemic, the incarceration of gang leaders in supermax prisons, and exhaustion of gang members with the gang wars of the 1990s but, most of all, the demolition of major Chicago housing projects, which resulted in moving youth into other neighborhoods.[217] The good news is that the demise of traditional gang leadership structures and loyalties presents substantial opportunities to guide youth into pro-social activities.

Urban violence today is often the result of individual reactions to a shooting of a peer or family member but may also be viewed as a response to an affront to neighborhood identity. Group dynamics reinforce the need to respond. The notion of "having someone's back" plays a major role in retaliatory violence. Retaliation today is often personal and linked to neighborhood loyalties and friendships, not directed by gang leaders. Violence is validated as some people are revered for resorting to extreme violence.[218]

Studies of youth in both New York and Chicago concluded that cynicism toward the police is of such a magnitude in certain communities of color that youth often see the police as more a part of the problem than a solution.[219] This situation contributes to violence as these youth believe that they have to take "justice" into their own hands. This situation calls out for substantial police reform to counter the cynicism and allow the police to play a more positive role.

Combatting the Social and Psychological Conditions Underlying Gun Violence

The work of Rachel Swaner and her colleagues at the Center for Court Innovation in New York City helps explain why gun violence and mass shootings cannot be tackled effectively without addressing the social, economic, and cultural conditions prevailing in some of the country's most violent neighborhoods.[220] These neighborhoods are disproportionately inhabited by people of color and account for a majority of the mass shootings in the US. Swaner and her team went to great lengths to establish contacts with 330 young men—mostly Black and Latino—in the Brownsville section of Brooklyn, Morrisania in the Bronx, and East Harlem in Manhattan. These men, many of whom are deeply involved in violence and criminal activity, are usually inaccessible to researchers.

Unlike the high-profile, high-casualty mass shootings the public is most likely to be aware of, such as those in Las Vegas, Orlando, Newtown, Parkland, Dayton, and El Paso, the young men in these neighborhoods tend to obtain their guns through personal networks rather than licensed dealers. Many of these guns are brought to New York from Virginia, South Carolina, and other southern states. New York state already has fairly strict gun laws, but in street purchases there are no background checks to determine whether an individual, by virtue of age or criminal record, is prohibited from gun ownership. Thus, tightening gun laws, especially locally, will have less of an impact with these men than in the case of the smaller number of high-profile, high-casualty shootings where guns have often been obtained legally.

The New York City study found that fear and actual violent victimization were key factors in gun carrying and that most of the youth were involved with gangs/crews at some point. Eighty-one percent had been shot or shot at and many had witnessed others being shot. Gangs offer protection in dangerous environments, as well as emotional support, and even financial opportunities. Most of those interviewed considered their neighborhoods as high-crime places and nearly three-quarters stated that they heard gunshots on a regular basis—at least monthly. Most owned or carried guns at some point.

Some of the youth carried guns because of their belief that they could face danger or retaliation at any time. Some mentioned a fear of the police. Said a 24-year-old Black man: "You gotta protect your life because the cops might shoot you." A 21-year-old said: "I got to keep my gun. Cops want to kill me. Dudes want to kill me. I don't know if I'll be alive tomorrow."[221] Another youth mentions the code that requires an individual to retaliate if their friends are hurt: "I have to carry one [a gun]. I got beefs. They shoot at my friends. So I have to shoot back."

Some of the youth reported they felt powerful with a gun. They also explained that being territorial in defending their neighborhood gave them a sense of ownership over their home turf when actual home ownership was unlikely: "We shoot each other over land that is not ours. It's feeling that you want to have something. We don't own a house. We don't pay the rent. But this is my block and you can't come here."[222]

While mass shootings occur throughout the country and in communities of all sizes, they are more concentrated in certain urban centers. As seen in Chapter 5, the 13 cities with the largest number of mass shootings account for nearly a third of all the mass shootings in America. Many of these cities will have a small number of neighborhoods in which many of these shootings occur and they are likely to share some of the characteristics seen in New York City's most violent neighborhoods. These common features include:

1. Guns are usually bought through personal networks rather than licensed dealers; therefore, simply focusing on tightening gun laws is not sufficient as violent youth in these neighborhoods get around the background check system when they acquire their guns.

2. In these high-crime areas, guns are usually purchased for self-preservation. Residents of these communities

tend to have a constant fear of victimization, are suspicious of the police, and feel the police cannot be relied on to protect them. Thus, the pervasive gun carrying and membership in gangs or cliques cannot be combatted without tackling the neighborhood conditions leading to gun ownership and gang membership.

3. The widespread fear and distrust of the police in these high-crime neighborhoods means that the police cannot be part of the solution unless they reform themselves. A department focusing purely on law enforcement and suppressing crime cannot be a useful partner in neighborhood reform.

4. Hypermasculinity codes that have evolved in certain communities emphasize violent responses when an individual perceives that he has been insulted or a friend, fellow gang member, or family member has been hurt. Such codes and the neighborhood conditions producing them must be tackled to make inroads into gun violence and mass shootings in these areas.

Types of Shooters and a Five-Step Approach to Pacifying Them

Criminal justice scholar Thomas Abt identified four types of shooters in the research, including interviews, for his book *Bleeding Out*.[223] There are the Wannabes, young people who will kill for status or belonging. A second group, Legacies, are young men who grow up in families deeply entrenched in violence. Violence has become normalized for this group. The third group is the Wounded, individuals traumatized as a result of foster care placement, beatings, or sexual abuse. The fourth group, the Hunters, enjoy violence for its own sake. They make up a small percentage of gang members who are prepared to step up, kill, and actually derive pleasure from it.

Abt points out that most of the evidence-based approaches, such as focused deterrence and street outreach in violence interruption programs, try to turn would-be shooters' lives around using a five-step approach. While neighborhood social and economic conditions must also be addressed, this writer endorses these five steps in dealing with individuals at risk of violence.

1. First, those most at risk are identified and are contacted for the purpose of engaging with them;
2. Then, these individuals are stabilized (e.g., assisted with urgent services like food, transportation, and shelter) and provided some measure of safety;
3. Once they are stabilized, the programs help them with their distorted thinking, unsafe behavior, and their trauma. Abt points out that cognitive behavioral therapy has been shown to be especially effective in relation to anger management and in helping people develop the skills to resolve conflicts peacefully and to stave off peer pressure;
4. Programs tend to offer educational, job, and other opportunities that offer clients a better life.
5. Those who refuse help and persist in violence must be met with swift and certain sanctions. Abt writes:

> *When all else fails, unlawful violence must be met with lawful force. By this, I mean incarceration.... This is an unfortunate but unavoidable reality. There is no prevention or intervention strategy that works every time.... If we cannot turn would-be shooters away from violence, they may become bona fide shooters who must be separated from society. In public health, when all else fails and the danger of disease becomes too great, isolation and quarantine forcibly separate the sick from the healthy. The same is true for public safety.*[224]

7
Preventing Mass Shootings:
Reforming Gun Policies

Louis Klarevas, author of *Rampage Nation*, asks readers to imagine that they are planning a mass killing. Manufacturing and detonating bombs are beyond the capability of most of us and, on the other extreme, knives or blunt instruments simply lack the range to kill large numbers of people and require that the perpetrator get too close to potential victims, raising the risk that they will be thwarted by victims. Firearms seem ideal for the task. Klarevas explains:

Irate perpetrators or vulnerable targets on their own don't necessarily result in mass murder. The key to killing on a large scale is the instrument of force employed. And, looking at the slew of recent slaughters, the lethal factor that nearly all have in common is the weapon. Quite simply, guns are at the root of most of today's deadly rampages. Guns prime the perpetrators. Guns penetrate the targets. And guns produce the carnage.[225]

Klarevas' observations are consistent with numerous studies over the last half century regarding the substantially higher lethality of guns when compared with knives, clubs, fists, and other instruments typically used in acts of aggression.[226] Emergency room doctors and surgeons treating bullet wounds agree that the laws of physics apply in understanding the lethality of different weapons, including differences among varying categories of firearms. Arthur Kellermann, formerly an emergency room physician and the founding chairman of Emory University's Department of Emergency Medicine, made the following observations on the factors that make guns and ammunition more or less lethal:

The specific capacity of a firearm to cause injury depends on its accuracy, the rate of fire, muzzle velocity, and specific characteristics of the projectile [bullet]...weapons with high muzzle velocities, e.g., hunting rifles, generally cause greater tissue damage than weapons with lower muzzle velocities, e.g., handguns. However, the size, shape, and nature of the projectile also play a powerful role in determining the severity of the resultant injury. A slower bullet, designed to mushroom or fragment on impact, may damage a much larger amount of tissue through direct trauma, cavitation, and shock wave effects.... Damage also increases in direct proportion to the mass of the projectile. The number of projectiles striking the body also influences the expected severity of injury.[227]

An analysis conducted by Rahul Mukherjee for the *Los Angeles Times* found that many mass shootings could have been prevented had the following five gun-related policies been in place: ban on straw purchases; safe storage requirements; assault weapons ban; mandatory background checks; and red flag laws.[228] Using data obtained from *The Violence Project* covering shootings with four or more fatalities occurring from 1966 to 2019, Mukherjee found that 146 out of 167 shootings (87%) could have been prevented, a staggering amount that would have spared the US a great deal of lost lives and much trauma. For example, a complete ban on straw purchases would have kept the two young shooters—both minors—at Columbine High School from obtaining an assault-style pistol from an older friend who purchased it at a gun show. In another example, national safe storage requirements could have made it more difficult for several other school shooters to obtain their firearms from home.

Mukherjee does acknowledge that there is no guarantee that determined shooters would have been prevented from achieving their goals. Safe storage, mandatory background checks, and other laws, for example, are not always complied with or enforced. Mandatory background checks can be circumvented through noncompliance (e.g., purchasing guns on the street); however, enacting these laws creates consequences for failing to comply with requirements.

A study for the advocacy group Guns Down America found that over half of the deadliest mass shootings during the years 2013–2018 could have been prevented through a national licensing system.[229] Such a system would provide law enforcement with discretion to prohibit an individual from acquiring a firearm, require that applicants file an in-person application to the licensing authority, include a waiting period, and mandate gun safety training.

Paul Reeping of Columbia University and his associates examined the impact of state gun law permissiveness and state gun ownership on rates of mass shootings.[230] The state ratings with regard to gun law permissiveness were obtained from *The Traveler's Guide to the Firearm Laws of the Fifty States*. The researchers found that a 10-unit increase in state gun law permissiveness was associated with an 11.5% higher rate of mass shootings. The authors also found that a 10% increase in state gun ownership was associated with a 35.1% higher rate of mass shootings.

Michael Siegel of Boston University's School of Public Health and his associates examined the relationship between state firearm laws and the incidence and severity of mass public shootings in the US from 1976–2018.[231] Specifically, they explored the issue of whether states requiring licenses to purchase firearms would have fewer mass shootings than those not requiring permits. They also examined the impact of a ban on high-capacity ammunition magazines on the number of victims of mass public shootings. The researchers found that state laws requiring a permit to purchase a firearm were associated with 60% lower odds of a mass public shooting occurring than states not requiring such a permit. High-capacity magazine bans were associated with 38% fewer fatalities and 77% fewer nonfatal injuries when mass shootings occurred.

Policies That Can Prevent Mass Shootings

The previous section showed that certain gun law reforms can potentially reduce the number of mass shootings. Based on experience from the US and other countries, this writer proposes the following gun policy reforms.

Licensing of Gun Owners

Virtually all advanced countries, other than the US, have some version of a licensing system for gun owners. Some require different permits for firearms of varying degree of dangerousness (Australia), with more lethal weapons being subject to stricter requirements. Others (Germany) confer licenses based on the uses of firearms, such as hunting, marksmanship, and gun collection. The US' National Instant Criminal Background Check System (NICS) is a rapid (typically a few minutes) system triggered by licensed dealers at the time of sale. Federal law currently requires no background check for private sales and many states fail to forward criminal, drug-related, and/or mental health information to NICS. Therefore, many checks are incomplete. Nationally, there is no direct contact between a gun buyer and law enforcement. In addition, individuals purchasing guns do not have to demonstrate any proficiency in the handling of firearms or any knowledge regarding legitimate uses of force by civilians.

Due to the flaws in the current background check system and the focus on a gun purchaser's criminal record, many of the most notorious mass shooters passed checks as a result of an absence of a criminal conviction even though they may have exhibited many disturbing behaviors. In a study covering 1984 to 2017, researchers at Johns Hopkins University found that handgun purchaser licensing laws were among the most effective in reducing mass shootings as they reduced a state's incidents of fatal incidents by 56% relative to states without such laws.[232]

Licensing laws are likely to have more of an impact on would-be shooters who purchase firearms through legal channels and who do not have easy access to guns through informal networks. To be most effective, the licensing system would be a national one as state licensing systems will be less effective when purchasers can get around the system by buying in a bordering state. For example, many guns used in crime in Chicago are purchased nearby in Indiana.

The licensing system should include the following features:

- Everyone who buys, owns, or possesses a firearm would be subject to the licensing system. Minors allowed to possess guns would at all times be under the supervision of a licensed individual;
- Law enforcement would conduct an in-person interview with every license applicant;
- A careful review would be conducted of the applicant's criminal, military, and mental health records;
- All firearm transactions, including among private parties, must be conducted through licensed dealers who are to ensure that the prospective buyer has a firearms license;
- Personal and work-related references would be interviewed;
- Training, including knowledge of the law relating to the use of force, safe handling, and storage of firearms, marksmanship, and judgment would be required from an accredited law enforcement agency with written and performance-based tests;
- A minimum waiting period of 15 business days for a license would be established to allow for a "cooling off" period for those who may be in the midst of a personal crisis and to allow sufficient time to undertake comprehensive screening and training of applicants;
- The license would be renewable every five years;
- Licensing would be retroactive, requiring current gun owners to complete the licensing process;
    - Applicants would pay a fee to support the licensing process.

Assault Weapons and High-Capacity Magazine Ban

Military-style assault weapons and high-capacity ammunition magazines have been used in many of the deadliest mass shootings in America. Our study of incidents in 2019–2020 shows that assault rifles are far more likely to be used in mass shootings than in murders overall. Firearms like the AR-15 are light, fire high-velocity rounds that shred body organs, and have features like pistol grips that make it easier to control the gun. High-capacity magazines allow a shooter to fire dozens of rounds of ammunition without reloading. Chapter 4 discussed the havoc created in a matter of a few minutes when an assault-style firearm is combined with a large ammunition magazine.

Many readers may argue that this country will never support laws banning these weapons and the magazines that feed them. In fact, such a law was enacted in 1994 but was allowed to expire 10 years later. One of the weaknesses of the law was the "grandfathering" provision that allowed prohibited models already manufactured to be sold. This left many of these weapons in the civilian market. Despite this loophole and other shortcomings of the law, one study of the ban showed that it was associated with a substantial reduction in the number of gun massacres (6+ people killed) and fatalities per incident when compared to the decade before and after the ban.[233]

Australia's sweeping ban on all semi-automatic and automatic long guns and its purchase and destruction of 650,000 of the banned guns has been highly successful. Following the nation's most devastating gun massacre in which 35 people were killed and 23 were wounded, Australia's federal government and states forged an agreement to harmonize gun laws, including the national ban mentioned above, as well as a national licensing system and a 28-day waiting period for gun purchases. Australia achieved these reforms despite intense opposition, a strong lobby, and a frontier history with a significant gun culture. There were 11 mass shootings in the decade leading up to the ban and no mass shootings in the decade following the ban.[234] In fact, the first mass shooting, a family murder-suicide, occurred 18 years later, and the first one in public occurred in the city of Darwin in 2019, 23 years after the national reforms.[235] Firearm homicides and suicides also declined following the national agreement of 1996.[236] It is hard to conceive of a gun massacre without the availability of the type of firearms banned in Australia.

In their study of fatal mass shootings for 1984 to 2017, researchers at Johns Hopkins University have found that states with a high-capacity ammunition ban face a 48% lower risk of fatal mass shootings than states without such a ban.[237] Columbia University's Klarevas and his associates analyzed state data on high-fatality mass shootings (6+ fatalities, excluding the shooter) from 1990 to 2017.[238] They examined the relationship between high-capacity magazine bans and both the incidents and lethality of high-fatality mass shootings. They controlled for 10 variables that might account for state differences in relation to mass shootings. The researchers identified 69 of these high-fatality massacres and found that attacks involving high-capacity magazines resulted in a 62% higher average death toll. States without a ban on these magazines had over double the incidence of high-fatality mass shootings and more than three times the annual number of deaths from these shootings than states with such a ban.

Some of the deadliest shootings (e.g., the Parkland, Florida high school shooting) were committed by young men who purchased their assault-style weapons legally. A ban would make this impossible. N. Cruz, the shooter in that case; D. Kelley, the Sutherland Springs, Texas, church shooter; and others would also have been ineligible to buy any firearm had a more thorough background check been conducted. Cruz had issued many threats and displayed many disturbing behaviors, in addition to his social media posts. Kelley had a domestic violence conviction in the Air Force, information that was not forwarded to the FBI's NICS system.

While it is true that some individuals determined to commit a mass shooting may have turned to illegal sources for their chosen weapon, others may have selected an alternative weapon that would have killed and wounded far fewer people. In any case, not all individuals have easy access to illegal markets, and the penalties associated with purchasing an assault-style weapon following a ban should deter some individuals. Another issue lowering access to prohibited weapons of war is cost. Just as with illegal drugs, the cost would be several times that of purchasing a weapon sold legally. Also increasing the cost would be the diminishing supply of prohibited weapons over time. Currently, a new AR-15 style rifle could cost up to $2,000. Following a ban, it would cost thousands more, making it unaffordable to young shooters of limited means.

Regulating and Cracking Down on Gun Carrying

America is not just an outlier in its number of gun owners; it also stands out, relative to other affluent countries, in the number of people carrying firearms. Millions of Americans carry loaded guns on a regular basis.[239] Since the late 1980s, states have introduced laws allowing people to carry concealed handguns. Currently, about 40 states are either "shall-issue" states, with limited or no discretion to deny a permit, or require no permit at all to carry concealed firearms.[240]

Gun carrying is especially widespread in some high-crime urban neighborhoods, where youths feel they are in danger from rival gang members, predators, and the police.[241] These guns are usually obtained through personal networks rather than licensed dealers. This situation is disturbing as ever-present threats and interpersonal or group conflicts can escalate to shootings and mass shootings when guns are present. As we have shown, mass shootings in 2019 and 2020 frequently fit this profile of conflicts that had escalated.

In the case of premeditated acts, the argument can be made that someone who sets out to kill will find the means to do so regardless of the weapons available. However, as was seen so often in the present study, many mass shootings are the culmination of road rage, a fight over a parking spot, a barroom fight, or an altercation at a party in which anger rises and may dissipate quickly. In such incidents, the weapons available at the time of a dispute will make all the difference for the outcome. Widespread gun carrying turns more everyday conflicts into homicides and even mass shootings. In the hands of impulsive youth who have lost all hope of thriving in society due to the economic distress of their neighborhoods, these weapons become even more dangerous.

Research shows that America's highly permissive right-to-carry laws, rather than improving public safety, have increased levels of homicide.[242] These laws limit what can be done as they provide authorities with little or no discretion in denying individuals the right to carry unless they fall in a prohibited category (e.g., felons, mentally ill). Ideally, national standards would be desirable to ensure a more thorough vetting of a person's suitability for gun carrying, and rigorous training is needed in the handling of firearms and the appropriate uses of lethal force.

Merely suppressing illegal gun carrying by itself does not address why young people are carrying guns in such large numbers in high-risk neighborhoods. As discussed in Chapter 6, the social and economic conditions creating the demand must be tackled. Researcher Thomas Abt points out that a strategy that purely cracks down on illegal gun carrying can alienate a community from the police and make it harder to enforce crime. Where police are viewed as lacking legitimacy, they lose their ability to enforce crime as the public withholds its cooperation as witnesses and conflicts are more likely to be settled through violence. Police crackdowns must be focused on specific behaviors and enlist the buy-in of the community by consulting with the affected community.[243]

This said, Abt points out that for a community to heal from violence, we must first stop the bleeding. One of the most successful law enforcement initiatives to reduce gun crime was conducted in Kansas City in 1995.[244] Police patrols were directed to hot spots where homicide rates were about 20 times the national average and there were many drive-by shootings. Officers focused their attention on detecting and recovering illegal guns through vehicular and pedestrian stops. Nearly 1,500 cars and people were stopped and 616 arrests were made. Guns seized rose by 65% over the previous six months and gun crime declined by 49%. A comparison beat several miles away showed no significant decline in gun crimes or seizures and there was no evidence that the directed patrols shifted crime to adjacent neighborhoods. Homicides declined significantly in the targeted area but not in the comparison area. Surveys of citizens showed that respondents in the target area became less fearful of crime and more positive about their neighborhood than respondents in the comparison area.

The Kansas City Experiment showed that the focused crackdown proved to be effective and perhaps the best way to deter gun carrying because many people carrying guns obtained guns on the private market, thereby circumventing background checks. However, the crackdown also showed that this law enforcement approach is not sustainable as the end of the program brought a slow return to the levels of gun crime seen before the program was established. Once the bleeding in the community is stabilized, other measures discussed in Chapter 6 must be available to address the economic and other concerns individuals have in order to steer them away from crime.

Safe Storage

Close to five million children live in homes where at least one gun is loaded and unlocked. In about two out of three school shootings, the young perpetrator obtained his guns from his home or from that of a relative.[245] Among the most recent examples of the potential devastating effects of a failure to secure guns was the 2018 murder of 10 people and wounding of another 13 at a high school in Santa Fe, Texas.[246] The 17-year-old shooter used his father's weapons. Inadequate gun storage also contributes to the theft of 300,000 guns each year.

Mark Shuster and his colleagues at the UCLA School of Medicine analyzed data from the National Health Interview Survey and found that 43% of American homes with children and firearms had at least one firearm that was not locked in a container and not locked with a trigger lock or other locking mechanism.[247]

In some countries, the safe storage of firearms—storing firearms unloaded and/or in a locked container—is a condition of gun ownership. In the US, there is an absence of national requirements relating to gun storage, and the majority of states have adopted laws enabling armed self-defense both in the home and in public places. Gun storage practices are weakening as more people are now keeping guns for self-defense, and many people have bought into the narrative that guns in the home make them safer. Safe storage is viewed by armed self-defense advocates as an impediment to those desiring quick access to a loaded weapon. However, there are many solutions that allow for both safe storage and rapid deployment of a gun.

The US General Accounting Office has estimated that close to a third of accidental deaths by firearms can be prevented by the addition of childproof safety locks and loaded chamber indicators that provide a visual and tactile (for darkness) indication that there is a round in the firearm's chamber.[248]

A recent report from the Rand Corporation shows that child-access prevention or safe storage laws may be among the most effective forms of gun regulation.[249] According to Rand, available evidence supports the conclusion that safe storage laws reduce self-inflicted fatal or nonfatal firearm injuries among youth and unintentional firearm injuries and deaths among children.

National standards should be established for firearm locking devices to ensure that they are both effective and allow for rapid deployment of weapons, bearing in mind the right of Americans to possess firearms for self-defense in the home. The federal government should launch a public education campaign to inform Americans about the extent of gun deaths and the benefits of safe storage, especially around children and teens. As part of the qualifications for gun ownership, owners should be educated about their responsibilities with regard to safe storage and informed about the most effective storage.

Following two high-casualty school shootings, Germany passed a law allowing authorities to conduct unannounced inspections of homes to ensure compliance with safe storage requirements.[250] It is hard to envision such a policy in the US; however, strong civil and criminal penalties ought to be considered where it is determined that guns used in crime became available to the perpetrator because a firearm was not properly secured.

Safe storage laws would be less likely to prevent mass shootings that stem from personal disputes in which perpetrators, including youth, obtain a firearm via personal networks rather than "borrow" one from a family member. Still, these individuals may steal firearms, and secured weapons are harder to steal. In addition, many weapons purchased through informal networks have also been stolen. Safe storage can impact the availability of guns on the street.

Regulating Firearm Dealers

Despite their lethality, firearms are among America's least regulated products. The Consumer Product Safety Commission (CPSC) is the federal agency that ensures that consumer products are safe. The CPSC regulates flammability standards for mattresses and it estimates that 270 lives are saved each year. It also regulates children's toys, appliances, and all sorts of household products in order to protect the public from harm.

However, unlike virtually every consumer product manufactured and sold in the US, the CPSC has been expressly forbidden by Congress from regulating firearms or ammunition. This was prompted by the fear of some legislators that allowing the CPSC to regulate guns would create a slippery slope leading to the disarming of Americans. Consequently, no federal agency has the authority to oversee the design of firearms to ensure they do not cause harm as a result of defects, even as more than 100,000 Americans are killed or injured by gunfire each year.

Guns used in crime and mass shootings are sometimes acquired from licensed dealers. Often, they are obtained through informal networks (e.g., on the street, from acquaintances). At other times, purchases are made through "straw purchasers," individuals with clean criminal records who buy guns on behalf of those who would be ineligible to do so due to a felony conviction or some other disqualifying condition. Some dealers are especially prolific in selling guns that are eventually used in crime. A 2000 report by the Bureau of Alcohol, Tobacco, Firearms and Explosives (ATF) revealed that just over 1% of federally licensed firearm dealers sold 57% of the guns later traced to crime.[251] For example, in 2005, 447 guns used in crimes were traced to a sporting goods store outside of Oakland, California. An astounding one of every eight guns sold in that store were later found to be used in a crime or were seized from an individual involved in crime.[252]

Gun shows are another major source of guns used in crimes. According to the ATF, 30% of guns involved in federal gun trafficking investigations have a gun show connection.[253] New York City investigators visited seven gun shows in Nevada, Ohio, and Tennessee.[254] They conducted integrity tests of 47 sellers, both licensed dealers and private sellers. Nearly two-thirds of private sellers approached by investigators failed the integrity test, selling weapons to buyers who said they probably could not pass background checks. Sellers are committing a felony if they know or have reason to believe they are selling to a prohibited purchaser.

More than nine out of 10 licensed dealers also failed the integrity test by selling to apparent straw purchasers. In all, 35 out of 47 sellers approached by investigators completed sales to people who appeared to be criminals or straw purchasers. Investigators also learned that some private sellers were in the business of selling guns without a license. For example, one seller sold to investigators at three different shows and admitted to selling 348 assault rifles in less than one year.

In America, there are more licensed gun dealers than grocery stores or McDonald's restaurants. Major flaws in federal gun laws impede the ATF from preventing the illegal diversion of firearms from licensed firearm dealers. The agency is limited to one unannounced inspection of a dealer in any year, and it faces an uphill battle in convicting dealers of wrongdoing. In criminal cases, it must show that the dealer *willfully* engaged in wrongdoing, and to revoke a license a pattern of wrongdoing over many years must be demonstrated.[255] Missing records can hide illegal sales; however, serious recordkeeping violations usually go unpunished. Since 1986, recordkeeping violations have been classified as misdemeanors rather than felonies, and federal prosecutors generally spend limited time prosecuting misdemeanors. As a result, most recordkeeping violations escape punishment.

The ATF simply lacks the resources to monitor the thousands of gun dealers across the country. The Department of Justice's Office of the Inspector General concluded that it would take the ATF more than 22 years to inspect all federally licensed dealers.[256] A *Washington Post* investigation found that due to inadequate staffing, ATF inspects the average dealer just once a decade.[257] The paper also reported that there are only about 15 license revocations in a typical year. Moreover, the Inspector General's 2013 report found that some license revocation processes took more than two years to complete, allowing scofflaw dealers to legally continue selling firearms during that time.

Gun shows are another weak link in the firearms marketplace. According to a report by the ATF, there are about 4,000 such shows a year in the US, as well as numerous other public markets (e.g., flea markets) at which firearms are sold or traded. Currently, under federal law, private sellers are not required to find out whether they are selling a gun to a felon or other prohibited person. If these firearms are recovered at a crime scene, it is very difficult to trace them back to the purchaser.

The ATF report notes:

> *The casual atmosphere in which firearms are sold at gun shows provides an opportunity for individual buyers and sellers to exchange firearms without the expense of renting a table, and it is not uncommon to see people walking around a show attempting to sell a firearm. They may sell their firearms to a vendor who has rented a table or simply to someone they meet at the show. Many non-licensees entice potential customers to their tables with comments such as, "No background checks required"... too often the shows provide a ready supply of firearms to prohibited persons, gangs, violent criminals, and illegal firearms traffickers.*[258]

A study by Mayors Against Illegal Guns found that states that do not require gun dealer inspections tend to export guns used in crime to other states at a rate that is 50% greater than states that do permit or require such inspections.[259] States with less regulation of dealers are also more likely to be the source of trafficked guns, as determined by the time it takes for a gun to be used in crimes following the initial purchase—two years or less is deemed to be an indication of trafficking. Another study found that state laws allowing or requiring inspections of gun dealers were associated with significantly lower firearm homicide rates than states without these regulations.[260]

Law enforcement operations against dealers in New York City illustrate how effective enforcement can alter dealer behavior, reducing the number of guns that are eventually used in crime. In 2006, the city launched a number of undercover operations and lawsuits, which could proceed under the Protection of Lawful Commerce in Arms Act if the dealer knowingly violated laws dealing with gun sales. Investigators identified 55 gun dealers in seven states who were supplying guns used in crimes in the city. About half of these dealers were caught facilitating illegal sales in an undercover operation and were subsequently sued by the city. Nearly all the defendants settled their case and agreed to modify their business practices. An analysis focusing on 10 of these dealers found that the change in their practices was followed by an 84% reduction in the likelihood that a gun sold by one of them would be later recovered in a New York crime.[261]

The ATF should have the authority and funding necessary to conduct routine inspections of gun dealers at its discretion. The agency should not be limited to one inspection per year. Sellers of ammunition should also be required to obtain a license. The Protection of Lawful Commerce in Arms Act, which grants virtual immunity to the gun industry from negligence-based lawsuits, should be repealed. Limiting the number of firearms an individual can buy at one time can potentially prevent an individual bent on mass murder from quickly acquiring an arsenal of weapons. Such a law can also make it more difficult for those engaged in gun trafficking. A policy of one firearm per 30 days should be adopted at the federal level.

A more vigorous enforcement regime targeting gun dealers and gun shows can keep many guns out of the illicit market, raising the cost of those guns that are available on the street. Increasing the cost of guns on the street may put them outside the grasp of at least some youth. Evidence presented in New York City, Chicago, and other cities shows that shooters in the most violent neighborhoods tend to obtain their guns through informal networks.

Keeping Guns from Dangerous Individuals

We have seen that individuals with a serious mental illness account for just a small fraction of all perpetrators of gun violence and mass shootings. More troubling are domestic abusers (including those in dating relationships), stalkers, individuals with impulsive and explosive anger issues, those communicating serious threats of violence, and substance abusers, especially those with a history of violence or mental illness. Domestic violence affects millions of people, and 4.5 million American women have had an intimate partner threaten them or a loved one with a gun.[262] Nearly one million women alive today have been shot or shot at by an intimate partner. Mass shootings, too, may have a connection to domestic violence.

Jeffrey Swanson of Duke University and his associates have found that about 22 million Americans (about 9% of the population) have impulsive anger issues (explosive, uncontrollable rage) and easy access to guns.[263] Close to four million of these angry gun owners routinely carry their guns in public and they are typically young or middle-aged men.

Aside from prohibiting at-risk individuals from purchasing guns, a mechanism is required to remove guns from individuals deemed to be dangerous once they have acquired guns. Individuals may become mentally ill, issue threats, or exhibit disturbing behavior that comes to the attention of family members, peers, or law enforcement personnel. A growing number of states have been introducing Extreme Risk Protection Orders (ERPOs), also known as "Red Flag" laws, that allow law enforcement and, in some cases, family members to petition a court to remove guns from individuals deemed to be dangerous to themselves or others.

An FBI study of active shooter situations between 2000 and 2013 found that the average active shooter displayed four to five concerning and observable behaviors, including signs of mental illness, problematic relationships, or an intention to commit violence. However, those witnessing danger signs did not notify authorities or authorities lacked the legal tools to intervene and seize the eventual shooter's weapons.

In May 2014, a young man shot 10 people in Isla Vista, California. He also hit seven people with his car and stabbed three more before committing suicide. Prior to this incident, his parents were so concerned about his behavior that they contacted his therapist, who informed police that he was likely to harm himself or others. The police interviewed him but stated that they did not have the legal authority to remove the shooter's guns or take him into custody. Following the mass murder, several states, including California, passed laws allowing the issuance of ERPOs.

States provide guidance to courts assessing whether a person is at an elevated risk of violence. For example, in California, the court must consider the following evidence:

- Threats or acts of violence, either self-directed or towards another, within the previous six months;
- A violation of a domestic violence emergency protective order that is in effect when the court is considering the petition;
- A violation of an unexpired domestic violence protective order within the past six months;
- Any criminal conviction prohibiting the purchase and possession of firearms.

California courts may also consider other evidence that is indicative of an increased risk for violence, such as the reckless use of a firearm, criminal offenses within the past six months involving controlled substances or alcohol, evidence of ongoing chemical abuse, and recent acquisition of firearms and ammunition.

ERPO laws differ from prohibited purchaser regulations that prevent specific groups of individuals, such as those with a criminal record, those with a history of domestic abuse, or those who have been dishonorably discharged from the military, from owning, purchasing, or possessing firearms. ERPOs can be served to anyone if the court determines that the person is at high risk for firearm violence, regardless of whether he or she falls in a category disqualifying him or her from buying or purchasing a gun. Typically, state ERPOs last from six to 12 months, but the person named in the order can request a hearing to terminate the order during the effective period. Some state laws also offer *ex parte* ERPOs, which allow eligible individuals to petition for an ERPO in emergency cases without waiting to provide notice of a hearing to the respondent. A preliminary analysis of 21 California cases in which mass shootings were threatened and ERPOs were issued found that none of the threatened shootings occurred.[264]

With regard to domestic violence, there is evidence that state laws prohibiting gun ownership by individuals subject to domestic violence restraining orders (DVROs) decrease total and firearm-related intimate partner homicides.[265] In 1994, Congress enacted the Violent Crime Control and Law Enforcement Act, which made it illegal to possess or receive a firearm where an individual is subject to a non-temporary restraining order protecting an intimate partner or the child of an intimate partner. In 1996, the Lautenberg Amendment extended the prohibition on possession of a firearm by domestic violence offenders to anyone with a conviction on a misdemeanor crime of domestic violence. The definition of an intimate partner under federal law excludes dating partners who have never cohabited and, therefore, many partners are not covered by these laws.

Some states have also expanded domestic violence-related prohibitions to include *ex parte* DVROs, which are short-term orders (typically 1–2 weeks) put into effect before defendants attend a hearing to defend themselves, thereby reducing the likelihood that a defendant will access firearms when the victim of abuse attempts to leave the abuser, the most dangerous point in an abusive relationship. Some states also allow victims of stalking to apply for orders of protection that bar firearms, and some impose firearm prohibitions to those convicted of stalking misdemeanors.

There is evidence, including from the present study, that some mass shooters have a history of domestic violence. As a result, prohibitions associated with domestic violence could disarm potential shooters and prevent mass shootings.

In addition to prohibiting firearm possession by individuals subject to DVROs, close to half the states require or empower judges to order these individuals to surrender their firearms. Despite evidence that laws establishing firearm prohibitions for persons subject to DVROs reduce intimate partner homicides, there is no procedure under federal law for the removal of firearms from these prohibited possessors.

It is recommended that federal firearms prohibitions include those meeting any of the following criteria:

- Individuals convicted of a violent misdemeanor;
- Those convicted of two or more drug- or alcohol-related offenses (including driving offenses) within a five-year period;
- Individuals violating a restraining order issued due to a threat of violence;
- Those harassing, stalking, or threatening a dating partner or former partner;
- Individuals convicted of misdemeanor stalking;
- Those subject to a temporary restraining order. All states should establish a mechanism whereby family members or law enforcement can petition a court to temporarily remove firearms from a family member if they believe there is a substantial likelihood that the person is a significant danger to himself or others.
- The age of 21 should be established as the minimum age for the purchase or possession of a firearm. The present study has shown that far too many mass shootings are perpetrated by persons under that age.

Preventing the Spread of Mass Shootings

The full names of mass shooting perpetrators have not appeared in this book. As discussed in Chapter 4, one mass shooting may beget another through the process of imitation. Individuals may be stimulated to action when someone with whom they can identify commits an atrocity. Saturated media coverage presents numerous details of a shooting, thereby amplifying its impact. Some shooters have displayed an obsession with mass shootings in general or a specific shooter or event.

The Federal Bureau of Investigation has adopted the "Don't Name Them" campaign, the aim of which is to prevent mass shootings that imitate previous incidents by minimizing naming and describing perpetrators, as well as limiting sensationalism and refusing to broadcast shooter statements or videos. Also important is avoiding detailed descriptions of the perpetrators' rationale for committing the shooting. When the purported motives for a shooting are broadcast, the media may be inadvertently pointing out similarities between the shooter and others that may have otherwise gone unnoticed.[266] For example, broadcasting that a shooter took revenge after he was bullied for many years suggests that the shooting is a possible response option for others with similar backgrounds who are experiencing bullying. An in-depth discussion of shooters' motives may well increase the likelihood of imitation.

Another measure to prevent imitation of shooters is to reduce the duration of news coverage after a mass shooting. While there is a demand for information following an episode of mass violence, saturated or prolonged media coverage may be perceived as rewarding the actions of the shooter through notoriety, thereby also elevating the social status of the shooter. In addition, live press events immediately following a mass shooting might be minimized. Such events can heighten the overall level of "excitement" surrounding the event. Instead, information could be released via written updates.

Another suggestion is that news outlets present only the facts of a mass shooting rather than entertaining or dramatic re-creations of the event.[267] The aim ought to be to reduce the emotion of a "breaking news story." Rather, the plain facts of the event should be conveyed in a straightforward manner and sensationalism should be avoided. Finally, detailed accounts of the actions of a mass shooter before, during, or after a shooting should be avoided. Presenting the shooter's actions in graphic detail provides additional information on the shooter that might prompt imitation. Behavior is less likely to be imitated if only a minimum of detail is provided.

Final Thoughts

The public's view of a mass shooting is an incident in which a disturbed individual enters a school, workplace, or crowded space and begins to indiscriminately fire at people. While such events do occur, they represent a small fraction of all mass shootings, but they receive more than their share of media coverage. In reality, the more than one thousand mass shootings studied for this book and occurring in 2019–2020 showed that these incidents are highly varied with regard to their location, circumstances, motives, and weapons used. Mass shootings may be committed by individuals or groups and, while some involve the random selection of victims, many target specific victims although uninvolved third parties may be shot unintentionally or due to the recklessness of the shooter(s). In still other cases, mass shootings arise from a dispute that erupts spontaneously at a social gathering or other encounter.

Our analysis of mass shootings shattered the myth that most mass shootings are attacks in which an individual randomly fires at strangers and seeks to maximize the casualties. Where a reason for a shooting could be discerned, it usually was a dispute, whether ongoing or spontaneous, group-related, or between individuals not aligned with any group. A disproportionate number of mass shootings occur in disadvantaged neighborhoods and among people of color, especially African Americans. A source of confusion is that many of America's most notorious and deadly shootings have been committed by White people often residing in suburbs and small towns (e.g., Columbine, Sandy Hook, Parkland, Sutherland Springs (Texas), Aurora (Colorado)). While receiving a great deal of media attention, such attacks in which students, church attendees, or theatergoers are randomly selected make up a small proportion of all mass shootings. Mental illness, too, accounts for only a small fraction of all incidents.

Another lesson learned is that the definition of what constitutes a mass shooting is highly consequential as it determines the number of cases identified in a given time frame, as well as conclusions drawn. Most definitions have one of two casualty thresholds: four or more people killed (excluding the shooter) or four or more people shot (excluding the shooter). The Associated Press/USA Today/Northeastern University Mass Killing Database, which adopts the 4+ people killed casualty threshold, uncovered 19 incidents in 2020, whereas our source, the Gun Violence Archive, adopting the 4+ people shot (not necessarily killed) casualty threshold, identified 612 mass shootings. This is an enormous disparity as the GVA revealed 30 times more shootings. The AP/USAToday/Northeastern U. source found that mass shootings actually declined by 42% from 2019 to 2020, while the GVA found that mass shootings increased by almost 47% over the same period! The GVA's finding is consistent with other sources showing that serious gun violence has increased dramatically in 2020 in many US urban communities.[268]

As argued in Chapter 2, this writer cannot agree with the notion that the murder by firearm of four people is considered a mass shooting while the shooting of 20 people at a garlic festival in Gilroy, California in which three people were murdered is not because fewer than four people died. The term "mass shooting" suggests that we are looking at a shooting rather than a mass murder. Also, many people wounded in such incidents—the shooter used an assault-style rifle in Gilroy—suffer lifelong injuries and communities are forever changed following such a high-casualty incident.

This study supports the findings of other research pointing to a continuing increase in the number and lethality of mass shootings. The fact that mass shootings are an escalating threat is especially noteworthy as improvements have occurred in emergency medicine and in the survival rates of those suffering gunshot wounds. The Gun Violence Archive has reported more than a doubling of the number of incidents from 2014 to 2020. Chapter 3 has shown that the stresses and privations associated with the Covid-19 pandemic and the racial strife unleashed by police killings of unarmed Black civilians contributed to a dramatic increase in mass shootings in 2020.

Will this trend of increasing mass shootings be sustained? The year 2020 saw an average of more than 50 mass shootings per month or almost two per day. While January 2021 saw more mass shootings than January 2020, it is hard to imagine the totals for the summer exceeding the numbers for 2020, when the loosening Covid-19 restrictions overlapped with the unrest following the killing of George Floyd.

Our analysis indicates that, in preventing gun violence and mass shootings, the idea that society must choose between tackling neighborhood conditions underlying the violence or reforming gun policies represents a false choice. Poverty, racism, lack of opportunity, hypermasculinity codes, gang membership, and social isolation all steer people toward violence while guns provide the means to commit acts of mass violence. Focusing exclusively on gun law reform ignores the fact that many individuals in the most dangerous neighborhoods obtain firearms as they fear for their lives and do so through personal networks rather than from licensed dealers. Focusing exclusively on criminogenic neighborhood conditions ignores the role easy access to guns plays in escalating everyday conflicts to lethal violence. The present study has documented many cases in which a personal slight has led to a mass shooting because a gun was nearby. Gun violence and mass shootings can only be successfully tackled if both the social conditions that underlie violence and the easy access to guns by those at high risk of violence are confronted in tandem.

Notes

[1] G. Lopez and K. Sukumar, After Sandy Hook, we said never again. *Vox* (July 21, 2020). Available at: https://www.vox.com/a/mass-shootings-america-sandy-hook-gun-violence

[2] A guide to understanding mass shootings in America. *The Trace* (January 6, 2017). Available at: https://www.thetrace.org/2017/01/understanding-mass-shootings-in-america/

[3] J. Ducharme, A third of Americans avoid certain places because they fear mass shootings. *Time* (August 15, 2019). Available at: https://time.com/5653218/mass-shootings-stress/

[4] K. Palpini, Survey: 1 in 10 Connecticut residents personally affected by mass shootings. *Daily Voice* (October 7, 2020). Available at: https://dailyvoice.com/new-jersey/lyndhurst/police-fire/survey-1-in-10-connecticut-residents-personally-affected-by-mass-shootings/795652/

[5] P. Chin, A Texas massacre. *People* (November 4, 1991). Available at: https://people.com/archive/a-texas-massacre-vol-36-no-17/

[6] F. Norris. Impact of mass shootings on survivors, families, and communities. *PTSD Research Quarterly*, 2007, 18(3): 1–7.

[7] American Psychological Association, *Stress in America: Generation Z* (October 2018). Available at: https://www.apa.org/news/press/releases/stress/2018/stress-gen-z.pdf

[8] Interview of Garrett Graff on *PBS NewsHour*. Available at: https://www.pbs.org/newshour/show/how-these-september-11th-babies-now-voting-age-see-america

[9] R. Walker, Ban traumatic shooter drills in US schools, urge teachers. *The Guardian* (February 29, 2020). Available at: https://www.theguardian.com/us-news/2020/feb/29/teachers-call-for-ban-on-shooter-drills-in-us-schools#:~:text=%E2%80%9CShooter%20drills%E2%80%9D%2C%20in%20which,biggest%20teachers'%20unions%20have%20warned.

[10] H. Samsel, Teachers' unions say active shooter drills need reform to protect student mental health. *Campus Security and Life Safety* (March 5, 2020). Available at:

https://campuslifesecurity.com/Articles/2020/03/05/Teachers-Unions-Say-Active-Shooter-Drills-Need-Reform-to-Protect-Student-Mental-Health.aspx?Page=2

[11] T. Kingkade, Active shooter drills are meant to prepare students. But research finds "severe" side effects. *NBC News* (September 3, 2020). Available at: https://www.nbcnews.com/news/us-news/active-shooter-drills-are-meant-prepare-students-research-finds-severe-n1239103?utm_source=The+Trace+mailing+list&utm_campaign=f025b79db0-EMAIL_CAMPAIGN_2019_09_24_04_06_COPY_01&utm_medium=email&utm_term=0_f76c3ff31c-f025b79db0-112434573

[12] Morning Consult, How 2020 is impacting Gen Z's worldview. Available at: https://morningconsult.com/form/gen-z-covid-impact/

[13] Everytown for Gun Safety, *The Economic Cost of Gun Violence.* February 2021. Available at: https://everytownresearch.org/report/the-economic-cost-of-gun-violence/?utm_source=The+Trace+mailing+list&utm_campaign=25d53683d4-EMAIL_CAMPAIGN_2019_09_24_04_06_COPY_01&utm_medium=email&utm_term=0_f76c3ff31c-25d53683d4-112376797

[14] American College of Surgeons Press Release, New study documents increasing frequency, cost, and severity of gunshot wounds that require surgical intervention. Available at: https://www.facs.org/media/press-releases/2020/gsw-study-081020?utm_source=The+Trace+mailing+list&utm_campaign=9ee8eb9801-EMAIL_CAMPAIGN_2019_09_24_04_06_COPY_01&utm_medium=email&utm_term=0_f76c3ff31c-9ee8eb9801-112376797

[15] T. Gabor, *Confronting Gun Violence in America.* London: Palgrave MacMillan, 2016, p. 11.

[16] E. Grinshteyn and D. Hemenway, Violent death rates in the US compared to those of the other high-income countries, 2015. *Preventive Medicine*, 2019, 123: 20–26.

[17] M. Healey, Why the US is No. 1 in mass shootings. *Los Angeles Times* (August 24, 2015). Available at: https://www.latimes.com/science/sciencenow/la-sci-sn-united-states-mass-shooting-20150824-story.html

[18] N. Nehamas, "School shooter in the making": All the times authorities were warned about Nikolas Cruz. *Miami Herald* (February 18, 2018). Available at: https://www.miamiherald.com/news/local/community/broward/article201684874.html

[19] Associated Press, Vegas gunman Stephen Paddock inspired by criminal father's reputation. *NBC News* (January 29, 2019). Available at: https://www.nbcnews.com/storyline/las-vegas-shooting/vegas-gunman-stephen-paddock-inspired-criminal-father-s-reputation-n964066

[20] A. Tikkanen, Virginia Tech shooting. *Britannica*. Available at: https://www.britannica.com/event/Virginia-Tech-shooting

[21] P. Langman, Seung Hui Cho's "Manifesto" (July 29, 2014). Available at: https://schoolshooters.info/sites/default/files/cho_manifesto_1.1.pdf

[22] S. Almasy and H. Silverman, Shooter who opened fire in workplace where 5 died had lost his job, police say. *CNN* (February 16, 2019). Available at: https://edition.cnn.com/2019/02/15/us/illinois-active-shooter-report/index.html

[23] San Bernardino Shooting. *CNN*. Available at: https://www.cnn.com/specials/san-bernardino-shooting

[24] United States Secret Service, Protecting America's Schools. Executive Summary. National Threat Assessment Center (2019).

[25] Federal Bureau of Investigation, Crime in the United States, 2018. Available at: https://ucr.fbi.gov/crime-in-the-u.s/2018/crime-in-the-u.s.-2018/tables/expanded-homicide-data-table-4.xls

[26] G. Fields and C. McWhirter, In medical triumph, homicides fall despite soaring gun violence. *Wall Street Journal* (December 8, 2012). Available at: https://www.wsj.com/articles/SB10001424127887324712504578131360684277812

[27] G. Kolata and C. Chivers, Wounds from military-style rifles: "A ghastly thing to see." *The New York Times* (March 4, 2018). Available at: https://www.nytimes.com/2018/03/04/health/parkland-shooting-victims-ar15.html

[28] J. Howard, Gun deaths in US reach highest level in nearly 40 years, CDC data reveal. *CNN* (December 14, 2018). Available at: https://www.cnn.com/2018/12/13/health/gun-deaths-highest-40-years-cdc/

[29] A. Rostron, The Dickey Amendment on federal funding for research on gun violence: A legal dissection. *American Journal of Public Health*, 2018, 108(7): 865–867.

[30] W. Wan, Congressional deal could fund gun violence research for first time since 1990s. *Washington Post* (December 16, 2019). Available at: https://www.washingtonpost.com/health/2019/12/16/congressional-deal-could-fund-gun-violence-research-first-time-since-s/

[31] T. Gabor, *Confronting Gun Violence in America*. London: Palgrave Macmillan, 2016, Chapter 13.

[32] A. Kellermann et al., Gun ownership as a risk factor for homicide in the home. *New England Journal of Medicine*, 1993, 329: 1084–1091.

[33] *United States v. Miller*, 307 US 174 (1939).

[34] *District of Columbia v. Heller*, 554 US 570 (2008).

[35] Giffords Law Center, Post-Heller litigation summary. Available at: https://giffords.org/lawcenter/gun-laws/litigation/post-heller-litigation-summary/

[36] Washington University in St. Louis, Initiative on Gun Violence and Human Rights. Available at: https://law.wustl.edu/faculty-and-research/whitney-r-harris-world-law-institute/initiative-on-gun-violence-human-rights/

[37] Amnesty International, *In the Line of Fire: Human Rights and the US Gun Violence Crisis*, p. 5; https://www.amnestyusa.org/wp-content/uploads/2018/09/egv_exec_sum.pdf

[38] K. White, F. Stuart, and S. Morrissey. Whose lives matter? Race, space, and the devaluation of homicide victims in minority communities. *Sociology of Race and Ethnicity*, 2020. Available at: https://journals.sagepub.com/doi/10.1177/2332649220948184?utm_source=The+Trace+mailing+list&utm_campaign=2135bf4f33-EMAIL_CAMPAIGN_2019_09_24_04_06_COPY_01&utm_medium=email&utm_term=0_f76c3ff31c-2135bf4f33-112376797&

[39] National Center for Children in Poverty, United States Demographics of Low-Income Children (2020). Available at: http://www.nccp.org/profiles/US_profile_6.html

[40] Rand Corporation, Mass Shootings: Definitions and Trends (March 2, 2018). Available at: https://www.rand.org/research/gun-policy/analysis/essays/mass-shootings.html

[41] J. Wallenfeldt, Texas Tower shooting of 1966. *Britannica*. Available at: https://www.britannica.com/event/Texas-Tower-shooting-of-1966

[42] M. Ray, Sandy Hook Elementary School shooting. *Britannica*. Available at: https://www.britannica.com/event/Newtown-shootings-of-2012

[43] S. Campion, Two victims have died, deputy injured following Liberty Co. shooting (June 1, 2019). Available at: https://abc7.com/1-dead-liberty-co-deputy-shot-%7C-gunman-on-the-loose/5321381/

[44] Rand Corporation, Mass Shootings; L. Klarevas, *Rampage Nation*. Amherst, NY: Prometheus, p. 40.

[45] M. Follman, G. Aronsen, and D. Pan, US mass shootings, 1982-2020: Data from Mother Jones' investigation. *Mother Jones* (February 26, 2020). Available at: https://www.motherjones.com/politics/2012/12/mass-shootings-mother-jones-full-data/

[46] Associated Press, US mass killings hit a record high in 2019: "This seems to be the age of mass shootings." *USA Today* (December 28, 2019). Available at: https://www.usatoday.com/story/news/nation/2019/12/28/us-mass-shootings-killings-2019-41-record-high/2748794001/

[47] Everytown for Gun Safety, Ten years of mass shootings. Available at: https://everytownresearch.org/massshootingsreports/mass-shootings-in-america-2009-2019/

[48] The Violence Project, Reducing violence through research and analysis. Available at: https://www.theviolenceproject.org/about-us/

[49] The Violence Project, Mass shooter database. Available at: https://www.theviolenceproject.org/mass-shooter-database/

[50] Gun Violence Archive, Mass Shootings. Available at: http://www.gunviolencearchive.org/mass-shooting

[51] Gun Violence Archive, Past summary ledgers. Available at: https://www.gunviolencearchive.org/past-tolls

[52] Mass Shooting Tracker, Data. Available at: https://www.massshootingtracker.org/data

[53] Stanford Geospatial Center, Mass Shootings in America Database. Available at: https://github.com/StanfordGeospatialCenter/MSA

[54] L. Klarevas, *Rampage Nation*. Amherst, NY: Prometheus Books, 2016.

[55] Klarevas, *Rampage Nation*, pp. 72–73.

[56] M. Booty et al, Describing a mass shooting: The role of databases in understanding burden. *Injury Epidemiology,* 2019, 6:47.

[57] Associated Press, Police say a 17th person was wounded in Gilroy Garlic Festival shooting. *Los Angeles Times* (August 29, 2019). Available at: https://www.latimes.com/california/story/2019-08-29/police-17th-person-wounded-in-gilroy-garlic-festival-shooting

[58] P. Hermann and M. Brice-Saddler, Shootings in district surge as officials confront mass shooting that killed 1, wounded 21 at block party. *Washington Post* (August 10, 2020). Available at: https://www.washingtonpost.com/local/public-safety/shootings-in-district-surge-as-officials-confront-mass-shooting-that-killed-1-wounded-21-at-block-party/2020/08/10/6d5446f4-daff-11ea-8051-d5f887d73381_story.html

[59] A. Larson, Gilroy Garlic Festival mass shooting: 1 year later. Available at: https://www.kron4.com/news/gilroy-garlic-festival-shooting/gilroy-garlic-festival-mass-shooting-1-year-later/

[60] W. Krouse and D. Richardson, *Mass Murder with Firearms: Incidents and Victims, 1999-2013*. Washington, DC: Congressional Research Service, 2015, Summary.

[61] Gabor, *Confronting Gun Violence in America*, pp. 68–69.

[62] CNN Editorial Research, Mass shootings in the US fast facts. Available at: https://www.cnn.com/2019/08/19/us/mass-shootings-fast-facts/index.html

[63] L. Klarevas, *Rampage Nation*, pp. 72–73.

[64] F. Taylor, Gunshot wounds in the abdomen. *Annals of Surgery*, 1973, 177(2): 174–177.

[65] G. Fields and C. McWhirter, In medical triumph, homicides fall despite soaring gun violence.

[66] M. Roth, Gunshot wound care has improved dramatically. *Pittsburgh Post-Gazette* (July 23, 2012). Available at: https://www.post-gazette.com/news/health/2012/07/23/Gunshot-wound-care-has-improved-dramatically/stories/201207230154

[67] J. Wu et al., Stay-at-home orders across the country. *NBC News* (April 29, 2020). Available at: https://www.nbcnews.com/health/health-news/here-are-stay-home-orders-across-country-n1168736

[68] George Floyd: What happened in the final moments of his life. *BBC News* (July 16, 2020). Available at: https://www.bbc.com/news/world-us-canada-52861726

[69] F. Zimring and G. Hawkins, *Crime Is Not the Problem: Lethal Violence in America.* New York: Oxford University Press, 1997.

[70] Zimring and Hawkins, *Crime Is Not the Problem*, p. 106.

[71] Zimring and Hawkins, p. 109.

[72] A. Karp, Civilian Firearms Holdings. *Small Arms Survey.* Available at: http://www.smallarmssurvey.org/fileadmin/docs/Weapons_and_Markets/Tools/Firearms_holdings/SAS-BP-Civilian-held-firearms-annexe.pdf

[73] L. Beckett, Americans have bought record 17m guns in year of unrest, analysis finds. *The Guardian* (October 30, 2020). Available at: https://www.theguardian.com/us-news/2020/oct/29/coronavirus-pandemic-americans-gun-sales

[74] C. Alcorn, Gun sales in January set a new record after Capitol Hill insurrection. *CNN* (February 3,2021). Available at: https://www.cnn.com/2021/02/03/business/gun-sales-january/index.html

[75] Gabor, *Confronting Gun Violence in America*, p. 40.

[76] E. Fridel, Comparing the impact of household gun ownership and concealed carry legislation on the frequency of mass shootings and firearms homicide. *Justice Quarterly*, 2020, online. Available at: https://www.researchgate.net/publication/343164404_Comparing_the_Impact_of_Household_Gun_Ownership_and_Concealed_Carry_Legislation_on_the_Frequency_of_Mass_Shootings_and_Firearms_Homicide

[77] P. Reeping et al., State gun laws, gun ownership, and mass shootings in the US: Cross sectional time series. *British Medical Journal*, 2019, 364: 1542.

[78] GVPedia, *Mass Shootings in America: 2013–2019*. Available at: https://www.gvpedia.org/wp-content/uploads/2020/07/GVPedia-Mass-Shootings-Report-Final.pdf

[79] E. Shapiro, 26 shot in 32 seconds. *ABC News* (August 13, 2019). Available at: https://abcnews.go.com/US/26-shot-32-seconds-details-videos-released-dayton/story?id=64953910

[80] Everytown for Gun Safety, Mass shootings in America. November 21, 2019. Available at: https://maps.everytownresearch.org/massshootingsreports/mass-shootings-in-america-2009-2019/

[81] D. Hughes, 2020 is shattering gun violence records. We must act. *Washington Post* (July 21, 2020). Available at: https://www.washingtonpost.com/opinions/2020/07/21/2020-is-shattering-gun-violence-records-we-must-act/?fbclid=IwAR163s62kJ3mjN3sRQ2ovCG9q6UCsUJv-ZbSIabTnYEPhUfZGlKsDxVycSY

[82] Kolata and Chivers, Wounds from military-style rifles.

[83] Kolata and Chivers.

[84] D. Heath, E. Hansen, and A. Willingham, How an "ugly" unwanted weapon became the most popular rifle in America. CNN Health (December 14, 2017). Available at: https://www.cnn.com/2017/12/14/health/ar15-rifle-history-trnd/index.html

[85] A. Yablon, America's obsession with powerful handguns is giving criminals deadlier tools. *The Trace* (December 5, 2016). Available at: https://www.thetrace.org/2016/12/americas-obsession-powerful-handguns-rising-gunshot-lethality/

[86] B. Caswell, Dayton Police Chief Richard Biehl presents at US Secret Service Mass Attack seminar. *Dayton Now* (August 6, 2020). Available at: https://dayton247now.com/news/local/dayton-police-chief-richard-biehl-presents-at-us-secret-service-mass-attack-decision

[87] A. Braga and P. Cook, The association of firearm caliber with likelihood of death from gunshot injury in criminal assaults. *Journal of American Medical Association Network*, 2018, July 1(3). Available at: https://www.ncbi.nlm.nih.gov/pmc/articles/PMC6324289/

[88] E. de Jager, et al., Lethality of Civilian Active Shooter Incidents With and Without Semiautomatic Rifles in the United States, *Journal of the American Medical Association,* 320, no. 10 (2018): 1034–1035.

[89] United States Consumer Product Safety Commission. Available at: https://www.cpsc.gov/About-CPSC

[90] Gabor, *Confronting Gun Violence in America*, Chapter 11.

[91] Giffords Law Center, Concealed Carry. Available at: https://lawcenter.giffords.org/gun-laws/policy-areas/guns-in-public/concealed-carry/

[92] J. Donohue, A. Aneja & K. Weber, Right-to-Carry Laws and Violent Crime: A Comprehensive Assessment Using Penal Data and a State-Level Synthetic Control Analysis, 16 *Journal of Empirical Legal Studies*, 2019, 16: 198–247.

[93] Violence Policy Center, Concealed Carry Killers. Available at: https://concealedcarrykillers.org/

[94] Florida Department of Agriculture and Consumer Services, Division of Licensing (September 30, 2020). Available at: https://www.fdacs.gov/content/download/82618/file/Number_of_Licensees_By_Type.pdf

[95] T. Gabor, *ENOUGH! Solving America's Gun Violence Crisis*. Lake Worth, FL: Center for the Study of Gun Violence, 2019, Chapter 10.

[96] B. Montgomery and C. Jenkins, Five years since Florida enacted "Stand Your Ground" law, justifiable homicides are up. *Tampa Bay Times* (October 15, 2010).

[97] D. Humphreys, A. Gasparrini, D. Wiebe, Evaluating the impact of Florida's "Stand Your Ground" self-defense law on homicide and suicide by firearm: An interrupted time series study. *JAMA Internal Medicine*, 2017, 177: 44–50. Available at: https://www.ncbi.nlm.nih.gov/pubmed/27842169

[98] C. Parsons and E. Vargas, The Devastating Impact of Stand Your Ground in Florida. Center for American Progress (2018). Available at:

https://www.americanprogressaction.org/issues/ guns-crime/news/2018/10/17/172031/devastating-impact-stand-ground-florida/

[99] C. Cheng and M. Hoekstra, Does strengthening self-defense law deter crime or escalate violence? *The Journal of Human Resources*, 2013, 48: 821–853. Available at: http:// business.baylor.edu/Scott_Cunningham/teaching/cheng-and-hoekstra-2013.pdf

[100] American Bar Association, National Task Force on Stand Your Ground Laws. Preliminary Report and Recommendations, pp. 21–22.

[101] United States Secret Service, Protecting America's Schools. Executive Summary.

[102] J. Hanna et al., Alleged shooter at Texas high school spared people he liked, court document says. *CNN* (May 19, 2018). Available at: https://www.cnn.com/2018/05/18/us/texas-school-shooting/index.html

[103] M. Shuster et al., Firearm storage patterns in US homes with children. *American Journal of Public Health*, 2000, 90: 588–594.

[104] C. Crifasi et al., Survey: More than half of US gun owners do not safely store their guns." *Johns Hopkins Bloomberg School of Public Health* (February 22, 2018). Available at: https://www.jhsph.edu/news/news-releases/2018/survey-more-than-half-of-u-s-gun-owners-do-not-safely-store-their-guns. html

[105] A. Semuels, Chicago's awful divide. *The Atlantic* (March 28, 2018). Available at: https://www.theatlantic.com/business/archive/2018/03/chicago-segregation-poverty/556649/

[106] Semuels, Chicago's awful divide.

[107] Semuels, Chicago's awful divide.

[108] Economic Innovation Group, Distressed Communities Index, 2020. Available at: https://eig.org/wp-content/uploads/2020/10/EIG-2020-DCI-Report.pdf

[109] R. Putnam, *Bowling Alone: The Collapse and Revival of American Communities*. New York: Simon and Schuster, 2000.

[110] W. Davis, The unravelling of America. *Rolling Stone* (August 6, 2020). Available at: https://www.rollingstone.com/politics/political-commentary/covid-19-end-of-american-era-wade-davis-1038206/

[111] Davis, The unravelling of America; and I. Glink and S. Tamkin, A breakdown of what living paycheck to paycheck looks like. *Washington Post* (August 17, 2020). Available at: https://www.washingtonpost.com/business/2020/08/17/breakdown-what-living-paycheck-to-paycheck-looks-like/

[112] A. Fradera, Poverty shapes how children think about themselves. *Research Digest.* The British Psychological Society (May 20, 2015). Available at: https://digest.bps.org.uk/2019/12/03/the-psychological-impacts-of-poverty-digested/-poverty

[113] M. É Czeisler et al., Mental Health, Substance Use, and Suicidal Ideation During the COVID-19 Pandemic—United States, June 24–30, 2020. *Morbidity and Mortality Weekly Report* 69, no. 32 (August 14, 2020): 1049–57. Available at: https://doi.org/10.15585/mmwr.mm6932a1

[114] L. Santhanam, Youth suicide rates are on the rise in the US. *PBS* (October 18, 2019). Available at: https://www.pbs.org/newshour/health/youth-suicide-rates-are-on-the-rise-in-the-u-s

[115] R. Friedman, Why are young Americans killing themselves? *The New York Times* (January 6, 2020). Available at: https://www.nytimes.com/2020/01/06/opinion/suicide-young-people.html

[116] M. Heid, Depression and suicide rates are rising sharply in young Americans, new report says. *Time* (March 14, 2019). Available at: https://time.com/5550803/depression-suicide-rates-youth/

[117] Heid, Depression and suicide rates are rising sharply in young Americans.

[118] J. Twenge et al., Age, period, and cohort trends in mood disorder indicators and suicide-related outcomes in a nationally representative dataset, 2005–2017. *Journal of Abnormal Psychology*, 2019, 128: 185–199.

[119] M. Lindsey et al., Trends of suicidal behaviors among high school students in the United States, 1991–2017. *Pediatrics*, 2019, 144: 1187.

[120] S. Matlin, S. Molock, and J. Tebes, Suicidality and depression among African American adolescents: The role of family and peer support and community connectedness. *American Journal of Orthopsychiatry*, 2011, 81: 108–117.

[121] L. Chavis, In Chicago, a steep rise in suicide among black people. *The Trace* (July 25, 2020). Available at: https://www.thetrace.org/2020/07/in-chicago-a-steep-rise-in-suicide-among-black-people/

[122] J. Knoll and G. Annas, Mass shootings and mental illness. Available at: https://psychiatryonline.org/doi/pdf/10.5555/appi.books.9781615371099

[123] Associated Press, Transcript of letter purportedly sent by Binghamton shooter. April 6, 2009. Available at: https://www.syracuse.com/news/2009/04/transcript_of_letter_purported.html

[124] S. Fazel and M. Grann, The population impact of severe mental illness on violent crime. *American Journal of Psychiatry*, 2006, 163(8):1397–1403.

[125] C. Martone, E. Mulvey, and S. Yang, Psychiatric characteristics of homicide defendants. *American Journal of Psychiatry*, 2013, 170(9):994–1002.

[126] Knoll and Annas, Mass shootings and mental illness, p. 91.

[127] P. Applebaum, Public safety, mental disorders, and guns. *JAMA Psychiatry*, 2013, 70(6): 565–566. Available at: https://jamanetwork.com/journals/jamapsychiatry/fullarticle/1674804

[128] Knoll and Annas, Mass shootings and mental illness.

[129] S. Kovaleski, Suspect in Virginia Beach shooting was a longtime city employee. *The New York Times* (June 1, 2019). Available at: https://www.nytimes.com/2019/06/01/us/dewayne-craddock-virginia.html

[130] Knoll and Annas, Mass shootings and mental illness, p. 89.

[131] B. Carey, Are mass murderers insane? Usually not, researchers say. *The New York Times* (November 8, 2017). Available at: https://www.nytimes.com/2017/11/08/health/mass-murderers-mental-illness.html

[132] M. Fisher and J. Keller, What explains US mass shootings? *The New York Times* (November 7, 2017). Available at: https://www.nytimes.com/2017/11/07/world/americas/mass-shootings-us-international.html

[133] J. Meindl and J. Ivy, Mass shootings: The role of the media in promoting generalized imitation. *American Journal of Public Health*, 2017, 107 (3): 368–370.

[134] R. Holden, The contagiousness of airline hijacking. *American Journal of Sociology*, 1986, 91(4): 874–904. Available at: https://www.journals.uchicago.edu/doi/abs/10.1086/228353?journalCode=ajs

[135] D. Robbins and R. Conroy, A cluster of adolescent suicide attempts: Is suicide contagious? *Journal of Adolescent Health Care*, 1983, 3(4): 253–255.

[136] T. Niederkrotenthaler, A. Herberth, and G. Sonneck, The Werther Effect: Legend or reality? *Neuropsychiatry*, 2007, 21(4): 284–290. Available at: https://pubmed.ncbi.nlm.nih.gov/18082110/

[137] T. Miller et al., Imitative violence in the real world: A reanalysis of homicide rates following championship prize fights. *Aggressive Behavior*, 1991, 17(3): 121–134. Available at: https://onlinelibrary.wiley.com/doi/abs/10.1002/1098-2337(1991)17:3%3C121::AID-AB2480170302%3E3.0.CO;2-U

[138] Meindl and Ivy, Mass shootings.

[139] Meindl and Ivy, Mass shootings.

[140] Associated Press, Texas gunman had history of violence years before shooting. August 26, 2020. Available at: https://www.kbtx.com/2020/08/27/texas-gunman-had-history-of-violence-years-before-shooting/

[141] B. Carey, What experts know about people who commit mass shootings. *The New York Times* (August 5, 2019). Available at: https://www.nytimes.com/2019/08/05/health/mass-shootings-mental-health.html

[142] Gun Violence Archive, Mass shootings in 2020. Available at: https://www.gunviolencearchive.org/reports/mass-shooting?page=11

[143] R. Rosenfeld and E. Lopez, *Pandemic, Social Unrest, and Crime in US Cities*. National Commission on Covid-19 and Criminal Justice. September 2020.

[144] E. Badger and Q. Bui, The pandemic has hindered some of the best ideas for reducing violence. *The New York Times* (October 6, 2020). Available at: https://www.nytimes.com/interactive/2020/10/06/upshot/crime-pandemic-cities.html

[145] Badger and Bui, The pandemic has hindered some of the best ideas…

[146] A. Humphreys, "Paranoid about the pandemic": How Covid-19 brought the largest criminology experiment in history. *National Post* (August 8, 2020). Available at: https://nationalpost.com/news/paranoid-about-the-pandemic-how-covid-19-brought-the-largest-criminology-experiment-in-history

[147] ACLED, US crisis monitor releases full data for summer 2020. Available at: https://acleddata.com/2020/08/31/us-crisis-monitor-releases-full-data-for-summer-2020/?fbclid=IwAR0CjaX1CeKmhPM8OqX8yXtgBYWDJHPSF935hyorh7xhaRVc UQfNN8vUrQI

[148] R. Rosenfeld, *Documenting and Explaining the 2015 Homicide Rise: Research Directions*. Washington, DC: US Department of Justice, 2016.

[149] J. Eligon, S. Dewan, and N. Bogel-Burroughs, In the wake of Covid-19 lockdowns, a troubling surge in homicides. *The New York Times* (August 11, 2020). Available at: https://www.nytimes.com/2020/08/11/us/homicides-crime-kansas-city-coronavirus.html

[150] Eligon et al., In the wake of Covid-19 lockdowns…

[151] A. Humphreys, "Paranoid about the pandemic."

[152] J. Roman, Summer of rage? Summer of discontent? Summer at home. August 13, 2020. Available at: https://johnkroman.substack.com/p/summer-of-rage-summer-of-discontent?utm_source=The+Trace+mailing+list&utm_campaign=8c4e1baa88-EMAIL_CAMPAIGN_2019_09_24_04_06_COPY_01&utm_medium=email&utm_term=0_f76c3ff31c-8c4e1baa88-112376797

[153] World Health Organization, Age-standardized DALYs per 100,000 by Cause, and Member State, 2004. Global burden of disease: 2004 update.

[154] M. Fisher, Ten country comparison suggests there's little or no link between video games and gun murders. *Washington Post* (December 17, 2012). Available at: https://www.washingtonpost.com/news/worldviews/wp/2012/12/17/ten-country-comparison-suggests-theres-little-or-no-link-between-video-games-and-gun-murders/

[155] Zimring and Hawkins, *Crime Is Not the Problem*.

[156] Fisher and Keller, What explains US mass shootings.

157 J. Santaella-Tenorio, M. Cerdá, A. Villaveces, S. Galea, What do we know about the association between firearm legislation and firearm-related injuries? *Epidemiological Review*, 2016, 38(1): 140–157.

[158] E. Kaufman et al., Making the news: Victim characteristics associated with media reporting on firearm injury. *Preventive Medicine*, 2020, 141 (December). Available at: https://www.sciencedirect.com/science/article/pii/S0091743520302991

[159] J. Fox, M. Gerdes, and G. Duwe, The newsworthiness of mass public shootings: What factors impact the extent of coverage? *Homicide Studies*, 2020. Available at: https://journals.sagepub.com/doi/abs/10.1177/1088767920974412?journalCode=hsxa&utm_source=The+Trace+mailing+list&utm_campaign=0ccd6d2e6d-EMAIL_CAMPAIGN_2019_09_24_04_06_COPY_01&utm_medium=email&utm_term=0_f76c3ff31c-0ccd6d2e6d-112376797&

[160] FBI, Crime in the United States, 2017. Available at: https://ucr.fbi.gov/crime-in-the-u.s/2017/crime-in-the-u.s.-2017/topic-pages/tables/table-4

[161] D. Solomon, C. Maxwell and A. Castro, Systematic Inequality and Economic Opportunity. Center for American Progress, 2019. Available at: https://www.americanprogress.org/issues/race/reports/2019/08/07/472910/systematic-inequality-economic-opportunity/

[162] Reeping et al., State gun laws, gun ownership, and mass shootings in the US: Cross sectional time series.

[163] K. Gander, Most mass shootings last year were within a mile of places with lots of kids. *Newsweek* (September 8, 2020). Available at: https://www.newsweek.com/mass-shootings-2019-mile-places-kids-1530265

[164] Violence Policy Center, New data shows that one in five law enforcement officers slain in the line of duty in 2016 and 2017 were felled by an assault weapon. September 25, 2019. Available at: https://vpc.org/press/new-data-shows-one-in-five-law-enforcement-officers-slain-in-the-line-of-duty-in-2016-and-2017-were-felled-by-an-assault-weapon/

[165] FBI, 2018 Crime in the United States. Available at: https://ucr.fbi.gov/crime-in-the-u.s/2018/crime-in-the-u.s.-2018/tables/expanded-homicide-data-table-8.xls

[166] FBI, 2018 Crime in the United States.

[167] C. Barton et al., Mass shootings are soaring, with black neighborhoods hit hardest. *The Trace* (September 3, 2020). Available at: https://www.thetrace.org/2020/09/mass-shootings-2020-gun-violence-black-neighborhoods/

[168] FBI, Crime in the United States, 2018. Available at: https://ucr.fbi.gov/crime-in-the-u.s/2018/crime-in-the-u.s.-2018/tables/expanded-homicide-data-table-8.xls

[169] Associated Press, DA: Suspect says he shot up Long Island deli over remark. *US News and World Report* (December 14, 2020). Available at: https://www.usnews.com/news/best-states/new-york/articles/2020-12-14/owner-is-second-man-to-die-from-shooting-at-long-island-deli

[170] C. Morris, Man arrested in shooting that injured eight in downtown Nashville. *News 4* (November 8, 2020). Available at: https://www.wsmv.com/news/davidson_county/man-arrested-in-shooting-that-injured-8-in-downtown-nashville/article_81a139d0-21dd-11eb-ac17-7b4ad7238ae7.html?block_id=998420

[171] C. Prince, 4 shot at downtown Atlanta hotel. *The Atlanta-Journal Constitution* (October 12, 2020). Available at: https://www.ajc.com/news/4-shot-at-downtown-atlanta-hotel/PEZDBV3L5NFRNDXSH74ZHUDMZM/

[172] B. Miston and A. DuPont, 7 Shot at funeral home near Fond du Lac and Townsend in Milwaukee. *Fox 5* (September 30, 2020). Available at: https://www.fox5dc.com/news/7-shot-at-funeral-home-near-fond-du-lac-and-townsend-in-milwaukee

[173] Klarevas, *Rampage Nation*.

[174] US Secret Service Threat Assessment Center, *Protecting America's Schools*, 2019, p. 12.

[175] P. Baker and M. Shear, El Paso shootings suspect's manifesto echoes Trump's language. *The New York Times* (August 4, 2019). Available at: https://www.nytimes.com/2019/08/04/us/politics/trump-mass-shootings.html

[176] Everytown for Gun Safety, Ten Years of Mass Shootings in the United States. Available at: https://maps.everytownresearch.org/massshootingsreports/mass-shootings-in-america-2009-2019/

[177] Associated Press, Aurora, Illinois, gunman who fatally shot 5 vowed to kill his co-workers if he was fired. *NBC News* (April 29, 2019). Available at:

https://www.nbcnews.com/news/us-news/aurora-illinois-gunman-who-fatally-shot-5-vowed-kill-all-n999571

[178] E. Watson, One year later: Here are the takeaways from the Virginia Beach Municipal Center shooting investigations. *13 News Now* (May 26,2020). Available at: https://www.13newsnow.com/article/news/local/tragedy-in-vb/one-year-later-here-are-the-takeaways-from-the-virginia-beach-municipal-center-shooting-investigations/291-9b4a70e6-d183-4483-bd6c-73e08226acab

[179] E. Davies, T. Craig, and H. Natanson, Ex-girlfriend says Dayton shooter heard voices, talked about "dark, evil things." *Washington Post* (August 5, 2019). Available at: https://www.washingtonpost.com/national/police-chief-it-seems-to-defy-believability-that-dayton-shooter-would-kill-his-own-sister/2019/08/05/920a895c-b79e-11e9-b3b4-2bb69e8c4e39_story.html?arc404=true

[180] P. Murphy et al., Dayton shooter had an obsession with violence and mass shootings, police say. *CNN* (August 7, 2019). Available at: https://www.cnn.com/2019/08/05/us/connor-betts-dayton-shooting-profile/index.html

[181] G. Nunn, Darwin shooting: Why mass shooting feels unfamiliar to Australia. *BBC News* (June 5, 2019). Available at: https://www.bbc.com/news/world-australia-48522788

[182] D. Diamond, Mass shootings are rising: Here's how to stop them. *Forbes* (June 18, 2015). Available at: https://www.forbes.com/sites/dandiamond/2015/06/18/charleston-deaths-are-an-american-tragedy-mass-shootings-are-rising/?sh=a304ee6787b5

[183] W. Skogan and K. Frydl, *Fairness and Effectiveness in Policing: The Evidence.* National Academies Press, 2004, Chapter 6. Available at: https://www.nap.edu/read/10419/chapter/8#224

[184] V. Romo, Dayton police killed shooter within 30 seconds of 1st shot, police chief says. *NPR* (August 4, 2019). Available at: https://www.npr.org/2019/08/04/748111546/dayton-police-killed-shooter-within-30-seconds-of-first-shot

[185] MSD Public Safety Commission, Shooting at MSD High School. Available at: https://www.browardschools.com/cms/lib/FL01803656/Centricity/Domain/13726/MSD%20Commission%20Presentation.pdf

[186] E. Pilkington, Colorado theater shooting: A deadly attack delivered with brutal precision. *The Guardian* (July 20, 2012). Available at: https://www.theguardian.com/world/2012/jul/20/colorado-theater-shooting-deadly-attack

[187] US Secret Service Threat Assessment Center, *Protecting America's Schools.*

[188] B. McMullen, Do we have the technology to reduce our epidemic of mass shootings? *Security Informed.* Available at: https://www.securityinformed.com/insights/technology-reduce-epidemic-mass-shootings-co-5589-ga.1591797092.html

[189] L. Green Mazerolle, Using gunshot detection technology in high-crime areas. *National Institute of Justice Research Preview* (June 1998). Available at: https://www.ncjrs.gov/pdffiles/fs000201.pdf

[190] D. Lawrence, N. La Vigne, and P. Thompson, Evaluation of gunshot detection technology to aid in the reduction of firearms violence. DOJ Office of Justice Programs (2015). Available at: https://www.ncjrs.gov/pdffiles1/nij/grants/254283.pdf

[191] C. Ferretti and G. Hunter, Detroit to implement gunshot detection tech to curb violence. *Detroit News* (September 9, 2020). Available at: https://www.governing.com/next/Detroit-to-Implement-Gunshot-Detection-Tech-to-Curb-Violence.html

[192] M. Desmond, A. Papachristos, and D. Kirk, Police violence and citizen crime reporting in the black community. *American Sociological Review*, 2016, 81 (5): 857–876.

[193] D. Kirk and A. Papachristos, Cultural mechanisms and the persistence of neighborhood violence. *American Journal of Sociology*, 2011, 116(4): 1190–1233.

[194] R. Swaner et al., *"Gotta make your own heaven": Guns, safety, and the edge of adulthood in New York City.* Center for Court Innovation, August 2020, p. 7.

[195] J. Hagedorn et al., *The Fracturing of Gangs and Violence in Chicago: A Research-Based Reorientation of Violence Prevention and Intervention Policy.* Great Cities Institute, January 2019.

[196] L. Mazerolle, S. Bennett, J. Davis, E. Sargeant, and M. Manning, Procedural justice and police legitimacy: A systematic review of the research evidence," *Journal of Experimental Criminology*, 2013, 9 (3):245–274.

[197] Rand Corporation, Legitimacy policing in depth. Available at: https://www.rand.org/pubs/tools/TL261/better-policing-toolkit/all-strategies/legitimacy-policing/in-depth.html

[198] T. Abt, *Bleeding Out*. New York: Basic Books, 2019, p. 88.

[199] A. Braga and D. Weisburd, The effects of "Pulling Levers" focused deterrence strategies on crime, Oslo, Norway: Campbell Collaboration, March 4, 2012.

[200] Rand Corporation, Focused deterrence in depth. Available at: https://www.rand.org/pubs/tools/TL261/better-policing-toolkit/all-strategies/focused-deterrence/in-depth.html

[201] T. Gabor, *Enough: Solving America's Gun Violence Crisis*. Lake Worth, FL: Center for the Study of Gun Violence, 2019, p. 93.

[202] Giffords Law Center to Prevent Violence, Intervention strategies. Available at: https://giffords.org/lawcenter/gun-laws/policy-areas/other-laws-policies/intervention-strategies/

[203] M.G. Becker et al., Caught in the crossfire: The effects of a peer-based intervention program for violently injured youth, *Journal of Adolescent Health*, 2004, 34: 177–183.

[204] T. Cheng, et al., Effectiveness of a mentor-implemented, violence prevention intervention for assault-injured youths presenting to the emergency department: Results of a randomized trial. *Pediatrics*, 2008, 122: 938–946.

[205] Cure Violence Global, What we do. Available at: https://cvg.org/what-we-do/

[206] J. Butts et al., Cure violence: A public health model to reduce gun violence. *Annual Review of Public Health*, 2015, 36: 39-53.

[207] J. Jacobs, *The Death and Life of Great American Cities*. New York: Random House, 1961.

[208] Crime Prevention Through Environmental Design. Available at: http://cptedsecurity.com/cpted_design_guidelines.htm

[209] J. Roman, Reducing Violence without Police: A Review of Research Evidence. New York: John Jay College of Criminal Justice, 2020.

[210] M. Koch and K. Stowell, Kansas City revokes 9ine Ultra Lounge's liquor license after two shootings in 2020. November 4, 2020. Available at: https://fox4kc.com/news/kansas-city-revokes-9ine-ultra-lounges-liquor-license-after-two-shootings-in-2020/

[211] J. Hagedorn et al., *The Fracturing of Gangs and Violence in Chicago: A Research-Based Reorientation of Violence Prevention and Intervention Policy.* Chicago: Great Cities Initiative, 2020.

[212] R. Swaner et al., *"Gotta Make Your Own Heaven": Guns, Safety and the Edge of Adulthood in New York City.* Center for Court Innovation, 2020, p. X.

[213] Swaner, *"Gotta make your own heaven"*, p. 33.

[214] Hagedorn et al., *The Fracturing of Gangs and Violence in Chicago.*

[215] Hagedorn et al., *The Fracturing of Gangs and Violence in Chicago.*

[216] Swaner et al., *"Gotta Make Your Own Heaven".*

[217] Hagedorn et al., *The Fracturing of Gangs and Violence in Chicago*, p. 8.

[218] Hagedorn et al., *The Fracturing of Gangs and Violence in Chicago*, p. 15.

[219] Swaner et al., *"Gotta Make Your Own Heaven"*; Hagedorn et al., *The Fracturing of Gangs and Violence in Chicago.*

[220] Swaner et al., *"Gotta Make Your Own Heaven".*

[221] E. Sandoval, The city confronts a culture of guns. *The New York Times* (December 13, 2020), p. 34.

[222] E. Sandoval, The city confronts a culture of guns.

[223] T. Abt, *Bleeding Out: The Devastating Consequences of Urban Violence—And a Bold New Plan for Peace in the Streets.* New York: Basic Books, 2019.

[224] Abt, *Bleeding Out*, p. 108.

[225] Klarevas, *Rampage Nation*, p. 265.

[226] Gabor, *Confronting Gun Violence in America*, Chapter 4.

[227] A. Kellermann et al., The epidemiological basis for the prevention of firearm injuries. *Annual Review of Public Health*, 1991, 12: 17–40.

[228] R. Mukherjee, How many mass shootings might have been prevented by stronger laws? *Los Angeles Times* (February 26, 2020). Available at: https://www.latimes.com/projects/if-gun-laws-were-enacted/?fbclid=IwAR0hcwPSJ4qE0NT0dGt6sCFKOCeyGWNZboNfacOYhCUOR FGO55KQM3Xi-aE

[229] N. Wilson, *Raising the Standard for Gun Ownership: How Firearm Licensing Can Potentially Save Lives*. Guns Down America. September 2019.

[230] P. Reeping et al., State gun laws, gun ownership, and mass shootings in the US: Cross sectional time series. *British Medical Journal*, 2019, 364: 1542.

[231] M. Siegel et al., The relation between state gun laws and the incidence and severity of mass public shootings in the United States, 1976–2018. *Law and Human Behavior*, 2020, 44(5): 347–360.

[232] D. Webster et al., Evidence concerning the regulation of firearms design, sale, and carrying on fatal mass shootings in the United States. *Criminology and Public Policy*, 2020, 19: 171–212.

[233] Klarevas, *Rampage Nation*, pp. 242–243.

[234] P. Alpers, The big melt: How one democracy changed after scrapping a third of its firearms. In D. Webster and J. Vernick, editors. *Reducing Gun Violence in America*. Baltimore: Johns Hopkins University Press, 2013.

[235] G. Nunn, Darwin shooting: Why mass shooting feels unfamiliar to Australia. *BBC News* (June 5, 2019). Available at: https://www.bbc.com/news/world-australia-48522788

[236] S. Chapman et al., Australia's 1996 gun law reforms: Faster falls in firearm deaths, firearm suicides, and a decade without mass shootings. *Injury Prevention*, 2006, 12(6): 365–372.

[237] Webster et al., Evidence concerning the regulation of firearms design, sale, and carrying on fatal mass shootings in the United States.

[238] L. Klarevas, D. Conner, and D. Hemenway, The effect of large-capacity magazine bans on high-fatality mass shootings, 1990–2017. *American Journal of Public Health*, 2019. Available at: https://ajph.aphapublications.org/doi/full/10.2105/AJPH.2019.305311

[239] C. Ingraham, 3 million Americans carry loaded handguns with them every single day, study finds. *Washington Post* (October 19, 2017). Available at: https://www.washingtonpost.com/news/wonk/wp/2017/10/19/3-million-americans-carry-loaded-handguns-with-them-every-single-day-study-finds/

[240] Giffords Law Center, Concealed Carry. Available at: https://giffords.org/lawcenter/gun-laws/policy-areas/guns-in-public/concealed-carry/

[241] Swaner et al., *"Gotta Make Your Own Heaven"*; Hagedorn et al., *The Fracturing of Gangs and Violence in Chicago*.

[242] J. Donohue, A. Aneja, and K. Weber, Right-to-carry laws and violent crime: A comprehensive assessment using panel data and a state-level synthetic control analysis. *Journal of Empirical Legal Studies*, 2019, 16(2): 198–247.

[243] Abt, *Bleeding Out*, p. 137.

[244] Abt, *Bleeding Out*, p. 136.

[245] B. Vossekuil, R. Fein, M. Reddy, R. Borum, and W. Modzelewski, *The Final Report and Findings of the Safe School Initiative: Implications for the Prevention of School Attacks in the United States*. Washington, DC: United States Secret Service and the United States Department of Education, 2002

[246] J. Hanna, Alleged shooter at Texas high school spared people he liked, court document says. *CNN* (May 19, 2018). Available at: https://www.cnn.com/2018/05/18/us/texas-school-shooting/index.html

[247] M. Shuster, T. Franke, A. Bastian, S. Sor, N. Halfon, Firearm storage patterns in US Homes with children. *American Journal of Public Health*. 2000; 90(4): 588–594

[248] US General Accounting Office. *Accidental Shootings: Many Deaths and Injuries Caused by Firearms Could Be Prevented*. Washington, DC: US General Accounting Office, 1991.

[249] R. Smart et al., *The Science of Gun Policy*. Second Edition. Santa Monica, CA: Rand Corporation, 2020.

[250] T. Gabor, *International Firearms Licensing Regimes: A Study of Six Countries.* Ottawa: Public Safety Canada, 2013.

[251] Bureau of Alcohol, Tobacco, Firearms and Explosives. *Commerce in Firearms in the United States.* Washington, DC: US Department of the Treasury, 2000

[252] D. Hennigan, *Lethal Logic.* Washington, DC: Potomac Books, 2009, pp. 174–175.

[253] Bureau of Alcohol, Tobacco, Firearms and Explosives. Following the gun: Enforcing federal law against firearms traffickers. Washington, DC: US Department of the Treasury, 2000.

[254] The City of New York. *Gun Show Undercover: Report on Illegal Sales at Gun Shows.* New York: The City of New York, 2009.

[255] B. Siebel and E. Haile, Shady dealings: illegal gun trafficking from licensed dealers. Washington, DC: Brady Center to Prevent Gun Violence, 2007. p. 24.

[256] Office of the Inspector General. *Inspections of Firearm Dealers by the Bureau of Alcohol, Tobacco, Firearms and Explosives.* Washington, DC: US Department of Justice, 2004. p. iii.

[257] S. Horwitz and J. Grimaldi, ATF's oversight limited in face of gun lobby. *Washington Post* (October 26, 2010). Available at: http://www.washingtonpost.com/wp-dyn/content/ article/2010/10/25/AR2010102505823.html?sub=AR

[258] Bureau of Alcohol, Tobacco and Firearms. *Gun Shows: Brady Checks and Crime Gun Traces.* Washington, DC: Department of the Treasury and Department of Justice, 1999. p. 6.

[259] Mayors Against Illegal Guns. *Trace the Guns: The Link Between Gun Laws and Interstate Gun Trafficking.* New York: Mayors Against Illegal Guns, 2010.

[260] I. Irvin, K. Rhodes, R. Cheney, and D. Wiebe, Evaluating the effect of state regulation of federally licensed firearm dealers on firearm homicide. *American Journal of Public Health.* 2014, 104(8): 1384–1386.

[261] D. Webster, J. Vernick, Spurring responsible firearms sales practices through litigation. In: D. Webster, J. Vernick, editors. *Reducing Gun Violence in America.* Baltimore: Johns Hopkins University Press, 2013, pp. 123–31.

[262] The Educational Fund to Stop Gun Violence. *Domestic Violence and Guns in the United States: A Lethal Combination.* October, 2016.

[263] J. Swanson et al., Guns, impulsive angry behavior, and mental disorders: Results from the National Comorbidity Survey Replication. *Behavioral Science and Law*, 2015, 33: 199-212

[264] G. Wintemute et al., Extreme risk protection orders intended to prevent mass shootings. *Annals of Internal Medicine*, 2019, 171(9): 655-658.

[265] Rand Corporation, *The Science of Gun Policy.* Second Edition. Santa Monica, CA, 2020.

[266] J. Meindl and J. Ivy, Mass shootings: The role of the media in promoting generalized imitation. *American Journal of Public Health*, 2017, 107(3): 368–370.

[267] Meindl and Ivy, Mass shootings.

[268] J. Bates, 2020 will end as one of America's most violent years in decades. *Time* (December 30, 2020). Available at: https://time.com/5922082/2020-gun-violence-homicides-record-year/